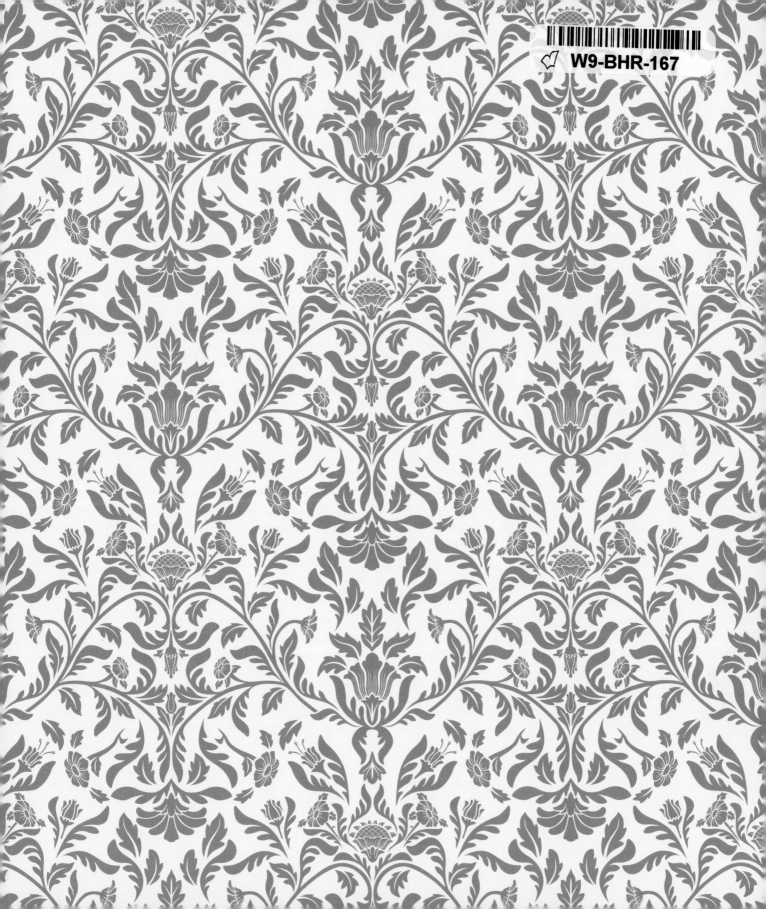

The VINTAGE TASTE

COOKBOOK

PRINTED IN THE UNITED STATES
by JOSTENS PRINTING
2505 Empire Drive
Winston-Salem, NC 27103
www.jostens.com

© Dewey's Bakery, Inc. 2007

Photographs 2007 Black Horse Studio

Design: Vincent Partners

ISBN 13: 978-0-615-16868-5

The VINTAGE TASTE COOKBOOK

Recipes
Jared Lee

Photography
Black Horse Studio

Food Stylists
Trey May & Robert Nicholas Pearse

Designer
Tim McCarthy

Editor
Brooke Smith

JOSTENS PRINTING

Contents

Salem Baking & Vintage Taste

vintage (vin´tij) *adj.* of a good period, choice, representative of the best

"Vintage" is the appropriate, if not the best, way to describe our family of products from Salem Baking. We began as a retail bakery in Winston-Salem, NC, operating continuously since 1930 as Dewey's Bakery. In 1992, we created Salem Baking Company to focus on traditional baked products that had potential for national distribution. We named our new company after the Moravian settlement of Salem located in our community, which was established in 1766 and was the source of the recipe for our first product: Moravian Cookies.

These legendary cookies have a story (see page 11) that spans generations and cultures. We are faithful to the origins of these time-honored classics. We bake in the homemade tradition and use the finest all natural ingredients. Because these cookies have withstood the test of time, they have become a part of our lives and the lives of many generations. They have a familiarity that transcends taste and time. They are tastes that provide more than passing satisfaction. They are tastes so vivid and distinctive, they have an almost metaphysical power to bring you fully into the present moment or transport you back in time to a warm and happy memory.

The Vintage Taste Cookbook introduces a new chapter in the story of Moravian Cookies. Their legendary flavors are now an elegant ingredient for cooking and baking.

Introduction

Cloves from Madagascar, Chinese ginger, Jamaican allspice, Indonesian cinnamon and nutmeg, Caribbean Key limes, Spanish clementine and Floridian Valencia oranges are just a few of the ingredients that create the distinct, delicious, and memorable flavors of Salem Baking Company's Moravian Cookies. Each of the recipes in our first cookbook features our Moravian Cookies--in some recipes as the signature flavor and in others as a subtle complement or a finishing touch. Made from many of the finest flavors from around the world, Moravian Cookies are now more than the perfect accompaniment to an afternoon tea or an evening cup of coffee. They also can be an elegant and easy-to-use ingredient for cooking and baking.

The finest ingredients, of course, are just one of the three requirements to create fabulous cuisine. Great flavorful recipes and careful preparation are equally essential. In that spirit, we also wanted to provide some inspired recipes that showcased the versatility of this new ingredient. To achieve just that, we enlisted one of the brightest, most creative chefs in our part of the country. His name is Jared Lee. Jared is the executive chef at Noble's Grille in Winston-Salem, NC, one of the finest and most popular restaurants in the Southeast (where Salem Baking is located). Jared specializes in the combination and blending of ingredients that produce flavors ranging from the sublime to the intense. A North Carolina native, Jared has had a lifelong immersion in the tradition of Moravian Cookies. This perfect combination of culinary skills and experience uniquely qualify him to author the recipes for our cookbook. He has created a wide range of recipes and organized them based on being relatively simple to prepare, perfect for any evening, or for those you may reserve for weekends and special occasions.

And no meal would be quite perfect without the perfect pairing. For special tips and wine pairing recommendations designed to enhance the flavors in every exquisite bite of each dish, we have enlisted one of the world's most renowned sommeliers, Christopher Sawyer. A Sonoma, CA-based wine expert, Christopher is a well-known wine critic, journalist and sommelier who travels the world in search of the very best wines.

Salem Baking is proud to introduce our legendary Moravian Cookies as an ingredient that brings many of the world's most cherished flavors to your kitchen.

Jared Lee | *Chef*

Jared Lee is a chef at the acclaimed Noble's Grille in Winston-Salem, NC. Born in Chattanooga, TN, Jared spent most of his childhood growing up in Wilmington, NC with his grand parents, where he first developed a love for food within the shrimping and farming communities of eastern North Carolina. Since he can remember, he's been farming and cooking with his grandparents--and throughout his career has been self-taught and trained by leading chefs throughout the Southeast.

Jared began working in the food industry at the age of 15, and the love affair continues today. From Cordon Bleu Catering to Chop House Restaurants, Jared held a number of positions before opening the George on the Riverwalk, where he was awarded "Best New Restaurant" by *Encore Magazine* for his melding of classic Southern cuisine with international influences.

Jared's influences? "I draw my inspiration for cuisine from my upbringing in the Carolina Low Country and my fascination with world cultures--from America to Asia, and everywhere in between," he says. On Jared's menus you'll find lamb chops over Israeli couscous, tabouleh alongside Southern collard greens or barbecued braised pork shank and black-eyed peas prepared au cassoulet.

When he's not in the kitchen, Jared enjoys wild mushroom foraging, martial arts, foreign languages, music and spending time with his daughter Adelae and his wife Heidi.

Note From The Chef

There is romance, even magic, in cooking. It is the possibility to transform ingredients into incredible cuisine, and incredible cuisine into delight–even cherished memories. Preparing a meal is an opportunity to experience both the joy of artistic creation and the joy of sharing that creation with others. These are the reasons I love to cook.

The secrets to success are simple. Plan your work. Thoroughly read over a new recipe to gain an understanding of the process. Carefully select your ingredients and necessary tools. Give yourself ample time to accomplish your tasks. Have an open mind and a creative heart, for no recipe is set in stone. Remember that recipes are open for your interpretation, and ingredients can be interchanged or omitted altogether at times. Most importantly, have fun in the kitchen and enjoy what you do.

I believe a dish should be an adventure for the palette, with contrasting and complementing flavors, textures, colors and aromas. You should involve as many of the different senses as possible, including sight in the use of color and aesthetic arrangement of the dish; smell in the aroma of the dish; sound in the different textures, such as the crunch of crusted fish; feeling with finger foods and textural changes within the food; and, of course, the food must taste great. You should also strive to touch on at least three of the five basic flavors: spicy, sour, salty, sweet and savory. Use these flavors to accent and elevate one another, adding richness and depth to your dish.

I've known Moravian Cookies all my life. They are more than cookies. These gems can be come flavor vehicles, textural components, sauce binders, crusting agents and garnishes for dishes we know and love. The recipes I have created come from regions throughout the world, with nods to Mediterranean, Asian, northern European and regional American cuisines. The story is in the spices. Some of the world's finest spices and flavors find their way into these dishes through the addition of Moravian Cookies. These recipes tell to life the rich history of the spices they feature; that includes the story of the beloved Moravian Cookie tradition. I am proud and pleased to introduce to you a new ingredient that will add both flavor and inspiration to your cuisine and bring smiles and fond memories to your guests.

Christopher Sawyer | *Sommelier*

A world-renowned sommelier, wine educator and critic, Christopher Sawyer travels around the globe following trends in wine and participating as a judge in international wine competitions. Sawyer is also notably the world's only Film Festival Sommelier, pairing wine selections with top films each year for the Sonoma Valley Film Festival in California's spectacular wine country.

Christopher is currently sommelier-in-residence at the Carneros Bistro & Wine Bar at The Lodge at Sonoma and serves as the private sommelier for some of the areas's most well-known residents, including the Getty family and Academy Award-winning director John Lasseter of "Cars," "A Bug's Life," "Toy Story" and "The Incredibles" fame.

Born and raised in the Sonoma County, Christopher is a well-respected journalist whose articles frequently appear in *Wine Enthusiast, Wine X, Wines & Vines, Wine Business Monthly, San Francisco Chronicle, AAA/Westways, California Wine & Food, Argus-Courier*, and many other national publications. In 2006, Sawyer opened the doors to Vine & Barrel, a hip international wine shop in the historic district of Petaluma, featuring more than 1,000 hand-crafted wines that can dazzle and delight the palates of a wide range of wine lovers.

Food & Wine Pairings

Since the inception of fine cuisine in Europe, the golden rule of working with wine has been to enhance, not overpower, the food being served. This technique is based on the idea that the two delicious parts of a great dining experience can co-exist and complement one another.

Today, the wonders of these magical sensory pairings are continuously in motion at classy restaurants around the globe. Yet, despite the growing accessibility of gourmet products and fine wines in the marketplace, there is still a lingering sense of intimidation surrounding the idea that these pleasurable experiences can be experienced in the homes of eager consumers. However, there is hope. In brief, the trick is getting to know the basic steps used by professional wine servers and sommeliers, myself included, to make these exciting gastronomical experiences take place in almost every situation.

This focus is made easy when working with the tasty delights featured in the Salem Baking Cookbook. Not only are these mouth watering recipes straightforward and simple to follow, but the Moravian Cookies and Crumbles and other natural ingredients highlighted throughout the book help add extra layers of spice, fruit and citrus flavors to make each delicious dish easy to pair with fantastic wines from around the world.

Rule One: Consider yourself a food expert. When you think about it, everyone has a list of favorite foods that they enjoy eating on a regular basis and other specialty dishes that they crave with the changing of the seasons. Much like these styles of cuisine, wine has its effect on the senses as well. For example, there are many light, crisp and fruity wines designed to refresh the palate in warmer months and heartier, richer styles of wine that warm the palate when the weather cools. Learning the art of pairing these wines with a wide range of fine cuisines can give you the power to complement and enhance taste-tempting dishes on a yearly basis.

Rule Two: Don't be afraid to play with food and wine pairings. There is a common belief that white wines only go with white meats and red wines only go with red meats. As a sommelier and journalist, known for traveling around the world, I'll be the first to say that pleasurable flavor sensations are not that limited. In fact, one of my favorite pairings is filet mignon with a medium-bodied chardonnay. The moral of the story is that you should not be afraid of experimenting with new wines. If it doesn't work, simply open another bottle!

Rule Three: The more dramatic the dish, the more dramatic the wine. In general, crisp, bright and expressive styles of dry white wines like sauvignon blanc and Pinot Grigio pair nicely with soft cheeses, fresh herbs, tangy salad dressings, citrus-based sauces, fresh oysters, mussels and other types of seafood. Fruity unoaked chardonnays with bright acidity go with chilled soups, salads, white fish and poultry; while buttery and oaky styles work much better with richer cheeses such as Brie, creamy soups, heavier sauces, roasted vegetables and meats. Conversely, Alsatian, German and domestic-style Rieslings, Gewurztraminers and Pinot Blancs with hints of natural sweetness and acidity, tend to balance well with spicy and savory foods.

Like the whites, red wines match best with a food of equal intensity. For instance, medium-bodied reds such as domestic Pinot Noir, Spanish Tempranillo, or Italian Sangiovese can accompany heavier seafood and lighter meats such as chicken, pork and rabbit, caramelized onions, mushrooms, grilled vegetables, and tasty sauces with cooked fruits. Heavier red wines work best with fatty foods: Cabernet Sauvignon goes with rich sauces, roasted and grilled meats; Syrah with seasoned lamb shank and venison; and a dense Barolo or Amarone from northern Italy with wild boar.

Rule Four: Pay attention to the detail of the dish you are preparing. Depending on the ingredients being used, the flavor profiles of the dish can be influenced by varying levels of sweetness, tartness, bitterness, saltiness, or unami–a Japanese term that refers to savory, mouthwatering flavors caused by naturally occurring glutamines commonly found in a wide range of foods, including tomatoes, asparagus, fresh meats, fine cheeses, and soy sauce. But once you identify these flavor sensations, it becomes much easier to select the appropriate wines to complement your meal.

Rule Five: Have fun sharing these flavorful experiences with your friends and family. When hosting an event at your home, a quick and easy way to stimulate the taste buds of your guests is to serve appetizers paired with sparkling wines, crisp whites, dry rosé wines or lighter fruit-driven reds. Tasty examples include: serving a chilled bottle of Fumé Blanc or a similar style of California Sauvignon Blanc with a hint of oak to complement flavorful Sweet Potato Crab Fritters (pg. 27) and the creamy mayonnaise, lemon juice and spicy capers used in the dipping sauce; a dry style of Champagne or sparkling wine to mellow out the salty flavor of dry-cured ham in the Prosciutto Wrapped Figs with Moravian Spice Cookie Crumbles and Chevre Stuffing (pg. 21); or a young Pinot Noir with a touch of spice to accent the earthy flavors of the Stuffed Mushrooms with Chicken Apple Sausage & Moravian Spice Cookies (pg. 23).

Starter Courses

Once they are seated, continue dazzling your guests' palates with seasonal starter courses. In spring and summer, the rule of thumb for salads is to make sure the acid of the wine and the food is balanced. A delicious example would be to serve the Spinach and Arugula Salad with D'Anjou Pears, Honey Roasted Peanuts, Moravian Spice Cookie Crusted Goat Cheese Cake and Raspberry Vinaigrette (pg. 31) with a chilled bottle of rosé wine from Provence or California. Not only do these hip new styles of dry pink wines compliment the fruit flavors of the salad, but the vibrant acidity on the finish balances with the vinegar used in the dressing.

In fall and winter, cold weather lends itself to serving hot soups and dishes with richer sauces. To highlight the natural sweetness of the flavorful Roasted Butternut Squash Bisque with Crème Fraiche and Moravian Spice Cookies (pg. 15), serve a fine German Spatlese Riesling with a tiny hint of residual sugar or a fruity Viognier. With the Seared Scallops on Endive Leaf with Exotic Herb Beurre Blanc and Macadamia-Moravian Key Lime Cookie Crumble (pg. 147), an elegant style of California Sauvignon Blanc or Spanish Albarino, a lovely seafood friendly style of white wine from the Rias-Baixas region on the Atlantic Ocean, pair nicely with the citrus and herbal notes in this versatile dish.

When working with casual entrées, the key is to select a style of wine that does not over power the dish. Serving examples include: a lightly oaked California chardonnay or a medium-bodied Italian red like a Rosso di Montalcino to complement the flaky texture of the

Moravian Key Lime Cookie Crusted Grouper with Lemon-Caper Butter Sauce (pg. 111); a smooth California Merlot to balance with the delicious notes of spicy Italian sausage, goat cheese, rosemary and sage in the Roulade of Chicken with Sausage-Apple-Moravian Spice Cookie (pg. 155); or a bolder California Cabernet Sauvignon or versatile Italian Barbera d'Alba to match the hearty flavors of the Sauerbraten (pg. 107), a classic German Style Pot Roast with Moravian Spice Cookie Sauce.

Sophisticated Main Courses

For more sophisticated entrées, use complex wines with balanced amounts of fruit, acidity and oak. Delectable examples include: Baked Halibut with Cashew-Moravian Tangerine Cookie Crumb Topping (pg. 153) with an elegant white Burgundy or Oregon Pinot Noir; Moravian Orange Cranberry Cookie Crusted Pork Cutlet with Roasted Apple-Sausage-Cornbread Spice Cookie Stuffing and Apple-Mango Chutney (pg. 57) with a fruity Italian Nebbiolo or more traditional Spanish Rioja; Osso Buco (veal shank steaks) with Fennel, Oranges, Green Olives, Israeli Couscous and Moravian Spice Cookie Sauce (pg. 164) with Chianti Classico or a well balanced California Cabernet Franc; and the Beef Tenderloin En Croute with Sausage, Shitakes and Moravian Spice Cookies (pg. 157) with a full-bodied California Cabernet Sauvignon or spicy Zinfandel.

Desserts

On the sweeter side, the effective use of Salem Baking's Moravian Spice Cookies and Spice Crumbles as important ingredients in the recipes adds more complexity, flavor and texture to the finished desserts featured in the cookbook. As a result, a wide range of sweet wines and ports pair nicely with these flavorful treats.

For example, the explosive flavors of fresh fruit and citrus in the White Chocolate Mousse Trifle (pg. 123) and Lemon No Bake Cheesecake (pg. 69) are further accentuated when paired with the natural sweetness of a late harvest Muscat from Europe or a Canadian ice wine. The lavish flavors of the Cherries Jubilee with Moravian Spice Cookie Whipped Cream (pg. 89) with the density of a late harvest California Zinfandel. And the savory flavors of the Moravian Black Walnut Cookie Crusted Torte (pg. 119) made with Chèvre, rosemary, honey, walnuts and pears with an expressive 10-year tawny port.

The British wine critic André Simone once wrote, "Food that is partnered with the right wine tastes better, we enjoy it more, it is digested better and it does us more good. No meal is ever dull when there is wine to drink and talk about." Not only can wine and food pairings create fine conversation, but they also can leave priceless impressions on the palate when executed properly!

Cheers!

Food & Wine Pairings

Moravian Cookies

The origin of Moravian Cookies is intertwined with the romance and intrigue of the great era of exploration and discovery by names like Marco Polo and Christopher Columbus. The ancient kingdom of Moravia, located in what is now the Czech Republic, was home to rolling hills dotted with castles and an ancient port nestled in the convergence of magnificent rivers. From this legendary port, ships would sail to the far reaches of the world in search of adventure and wealth. As they returned home, there would be both factual and mythical tales of their explorations and wonders that they had witnessed.

As captains would unload their rich bounties from these long voyages, exotic combinations of newly discovered, highly coveted ingredients were unveiled. Allspice from the Caribbean, ginger from China, cloves from the Malacca Islands, cinnamon from Ceylon, bourbon bean vanilla from Madagascar, and barrels of sugar cane from the West Indies became all the rage.

During the long voyages, sweet amber syrup would flow from the sugar cane and settle in the bottom of the wood barrels. This substance was discarded as waste until the incredible piquant flavor of the molasses was discovered. It then became one of the most valued and sought-after ingredients. Early attempts at blending these treasured flavors into traditional size, thick cookies were unsuccessful, as they were too hard to bite. Diligence and persistence prevailed, however, and eventually it was learned that rolling the dough paper-thin and baking slowly created a cookie with a pleasant, crisp texture that captured the intense flavors of the exotic spices they loved so much.

Over the ages, these thin cookies became legendary. Due to the expense and rarity of the ingredients, along with the incredible skill and time involved in rolling the dough to almost translucent thinness, they were only baked for special occasions and holidays.

More than 200 years ago, the people of Moravia, seeking religious freedom and a better life in the New World, made the long journey to the colonies of North America. Settling in North Carolina in 1766, they brought their recipe for the cookies that now bears their name. Since 1930, our bakery has rekindled the tradition of this centuries-old recipe.

Moravian Cookies

Featured Any NIGHT RECIPES

Salem Baking's quick and simple recipes require little cooking experience or time. These dishes feature simple ingredients and techniques that come to life with the vintage flavors of Moravian Cookies. From a classic roast chicken and stuffing to traditional casseroles, new family favorites are sure to be found.

Any Night

Roasted Butternut Squash Bisque

Made with Crème Fraiche & Moravian Spice Cookies

For the Crème Fraiche (must be made three days in advance)
Mix ingredients well and place in a very clean glass. Cover with a very clean, thin dish towel (cheese-cloth works best). Seal tightly with two thick rubber bands and let sit at room temperature for three days. Once set, there should be a little bit of clear or milky liquid at the bottom, a thick skin on the top, and the liquid should be noticeably thicker. Refrigerate three hours to set thoroughly. Scrape off skin with a spoon, and run a butter knife down the edge of the glass to the liquid layer. Tilt the glass gently to the side to let the liquid run out as much as possible. Reserve glass covered in refrigerator.

For the Soup
Place squash in a large roasting pan and roast in oven on 375° for 45 minutes. Add other vegetables and garlic and roast for an additional 45 minutes. Once vegetables are roasted and the squash is tender, use a towel to hold the squash and scrape the pulp off the skin with a spoon into a blender. Add the other vegetables, butter, cream, applesauce and puree until it reaches a smooth, creamy consistency (may need more or less liquid depending on consistency). Season with kosher salt and fresh ground black pepper to taste. Strain into a saucepan and bring to simmer over medium heat for 8-10 minutes. Reserve. Can be made three days in advance.

For the Plating
Pour soup into bowls. Top with a dollop of Crème Fraiche and loosely cracked Moravian Spice Cookies.

On Crème Fraiche
Crème Fraiche, France's answer to sour cream, is a versatile ingredient in the kitchen, stepping in for heavy cream, butter or sour cream in many recipes. Try fresh strawberries with Crème Fraiche and a drizzle of honey. Mix with chopped shallots, grain mustard and fresh dill as a sauce for grilled seafood, especially salmon. Add to mashed potatoes with Brie cheese and pair with a great steak.

Ingredients

For the Crème Fraiche
2 c. heavy cream
2 tbsp. buttermilk
(must say "with active cultures")

For the Soup
3 lrg butternut squash, halved and seeded
2 med carrots, peeled & large chopped
3 med parsnips, peeled & large chopped (optional)
1 lrg yellow onion, large chopped
2 ribs celery, large chopped
3 garlic cloves
2 tbsp. unsalted butter
2 c. heavy cream (or half & half)
1/2 c. applesauce
Kosher salt and fresh black pepper to taste
Moravian Spice Cookies

Butternut Squash Bisque

Moravian Key Lime Cookie & Coconut Crusted Shrimp

Made with Jalapeño Peach Preserves

For the Jalapeño-Peach Preserves
Combine all ingredients in a saucepan and bring to a simmer over medium heat. Cook 5-8 minutes to cook out the alcohol. Remove and cool to room temperature. The preserves can be made two weeks in advance.

For the Shrimp
Mix the cookie crumbles and shredded coconut in a bowl. Mix the eggs and milk in a separate bowl. Season the shrimp with salt and pepper. Dredge shrimp in the flour, then dip in the egg wash and then in the cookie coconut mix. Deep fry shrimp at 350° for 4-5 minutes until crispy, golden and cooked through.

For the Plating
Serve on a large platter with the preserves as an hors d'oeuvre or with slaw and fried plantains as an entrée.

Ingredients

For the Jalapeño-Peach Preserves
1 sm jar peach preserves
1 sm jar red jalapeño jelly
2 tbsp. cider vinegar
1/4 c. peach schnapps

For the Shrimp
3 c. Moravian Key Lime Cookie Crumbles
2 c. shredded coconut
2 eggs
2 c. milk
2 lb. 16/20 ct. shrimp, peeled & deveined
salt & pepper
2 c. flour
oil for frying

For the Plating
slaw
fried plantains

Coconut Crusted Shrimp

Pepperjack Crab Dip
Made with Moravian Key Lime Cookie Crumb Topping

For the Crab Dip
Combine all ingredients except crab and pepperjack in a mixer and mix until creamy with no lumps. Then fold in shredded cheese and lastly crab, being careful not to break up the lumps, then pour mixture into a 9 x 9-inch casserole dish.

For the Crumb Topping
Combine all ingredients and spread over the top of the casserole and bake in 375° oven for 20-25 minutes until golden brown.

For the Plating
Serve with an assortment of flatbreads, crackers or toast points.

Ingredients

For the Crab Dip
6 oz. cream cheese, softened
4 tbsp. sour cream
2 tbsp. Dijon mustard
2 tbsp. white wine
1 sm shallot minced
juice of 1/2 lemon
dash of hot sauce
dash of Worcestershire sauce
1 tbsp. Old Bay seasoning
1 tsp. fresh sage, chopped
1/2 c. shredded pepperjack cheese
2 lb. jumbo lump crabmeat

For the Crumb Topping
1 oz. unsalted butter, melted
1 c. Italian bread crumbs seasoned
1/4 c. Moravian Key Lime Cookie
  Crumbles
1/4 c. shredded Asiago cheese
1/4 c. shredded pepperjack cheese
1 tbsp. fresh flat leaf parsley, chopped
salt & pepper

For the Plating
crackers or toast points

Pumpkin Dip

Made with Moravian Pumpkin Spice Cookies

For the Dip
Beat all ingredients together with a mixer until creamy. Place in a serving bowl and refrigerate.

For the Plating
Serve with Moravian Pumpkin Spice Cookies on a platter for holidays, dinner parties or bring them to work and make new friends in the office.

Where is Moravia Exactly?
Moravia is an old part of the Czech Republic comprised of the three southernmost provinces, Olomouc, Zlín and Moravia-Silesia. Named after the Morava River that runs through it, Moravians speak Slavic and call Olomouc their capital. Most notably, Moravia was a vassal to Archduke Franz Ferdinand of the Austrian Empire, whose assassination caused the start of World War I.

Ingredients

One 15 oz. can pumpkin pie filling
8 oz. cream cheese
2 tbsp. cinnamon
1/4 c. brown sugar
pinch salt
Moravian Pumpkin Spice Cookies

Prosciutto Wrapped Figs
Made with Moravian Spice Cookie & Chèvre Stuffing

For the Stuffing
Combine all ingredients in a mixing bowl and beat with a hand mixer until creamy. Season with salt and pepper. Refrigerate.

For the Figs
Cut the stems off the figs and score the tops in a crosswise pattern almost to the bottom. Open the fig and place a small dollop of the Chèvre mixture inside the fig. Take a slice of the Prosciutto and slice it lengthwise in half. Wrap around the fig and secure with a small rosemary sprig or toothpick. Lightly oil a sauté pan with olive oil and bake figs in pan for 12-15 minutes at 400° until Chèvre is bubbly and prosciutto is well crisped.

For the Plating
Serve three of the roasted figs on a small bunch of baby greens dressed with balsamic vinaigrette and fresh cucumber slices. Drizzle figs with an aged balsamic vinegar. An alternate plating option could include fresh rosemary sprigs and small purple grapes, as pictured.

On Figs
Figs are considered to be one of the three trees cultivated in ancient times, along with the almond and olive. We know people were actively cultivating fig trees in ancient times, because the plant only fruits when hermaphrodized by human intervention. Fig fruit remains have been found in ancient ruins in the Middle East.

Ingredients

For the Stuffing
1/4 c. Chèvre
1/2 c. Moravian Spice Cookie
   Crumbles
3 tbsp. honey
2 tsp. fresh rosemary, chopped
salt & pepper

For the Figs
12 fresh black mission or brown turkey
   figs
6 paper-thin slices Prosciutto
olive oil

For the Plating
small bunch of baby greens
balsamic vinaigrette
cucumber slices
small purple grapes

Prosciutto Wrapped Figs

Stuffed Mushrooms

Made with Chicken Apple Sausage & Moravian Spice Cookies

For the Sauce

Crisp the bacon in a large sauté pan for 8-10 minutes. Remove and add the chicken sausage to the bacon grease. Brown 8-10 minutes, using a spoon to break up the pieces of sausage. Remove the sausage with a slotted spoon and drain on paper towels. Add the vegetables to the pan, along with the mushroom stems. Sauté 10-12 minutes. Add the apples and sauté until softened (4-5 minutes). Deglaze with white wine, chicken broth and herbs. Simmer 10-15 minutes until liquid is reduced by half. Add the cookie crumbles and mix with a spoon until liquid is absorbed and thickened. Add sausage, bacon, and 1/4 cup cheddar. Stir to mix ingredients well. Stuff mixture into mushroom caps and smooth tops with a spoon. Place in a small casserole dish. Top with remaining shredded cheddar and bake at 400° for 12-15 minutes until cheese is melted and browned.

For the Plating

Serve the mushrooms in the baking dish with toothpicks.

Ingredients

For the Sauce
4 thick slices Applewood smoked bacon
Four 6-8 oz. chicken & apple sausage links, casing removed
1/2 rib celery, diced
1/4 red pepper, diced
1 small shallot, diced fine
1/2 med yellow onion, diced
16 lrg button mushrooms, stems removed, minced & reserved
1/2 green apple, diced small
1/8 c. white wine
Half 10 oz. can chicken broth
1 tsp. fresh rosemary, chopped
1 tsp. fresh thyme, chopped
1/2 c. Moravian Spice Cookie Crumbles
1/2 c. extra sharp cheddar cheese, grated & divided

Stuffed Mushrooms

Baba Ghanouj

Middle Eastern Roasted Eggplant Dip

For the Baba Ghanouj

Brush the eggplants with olive oil and bake at 400° in oven until skin bursts and eggplant are extremely soft (15-20 minutes). Scoop the pulp of the eggplant into a food processor, along with all other ingredients. Process on high until smooth and creamy. Season with salt and pepper.

For the Plating

Serve the Baba Ghanouj in a bowl with a drizzle of extra virgin olive oil, a sprinkle of paprika, as well as a few toasted pine nuts and sesame seeds. Traditional accompaniments include flatbread, feta cheese, bell peppers, cucumbers, radishes, tomatoes and red onions.

Ingredients

For the Baba Ghanouj
5 sm eggplants (softball size)
2 tbsp. olive oil
1 med yellow onion, diced & sweated
   in olive oil until translucent
2 cloves garlic, minced
2 tbsp. tahini paste
juice & zest of 1 lemon
2 tbsp. fresh flat-leaf parsley, chopped
1 1/2 tsp. ground cumin
pinch cayenne pepper
1/4 c. pine nuts, toasted
1/4 c. Moravian Spice Cookie
   Crumbles

For the Plating
extra virgin olive oil
sesame seeds
flatbread
feta cheese
bell peppers
cucumbers
radishes
tomatoes
red onions

Honey Orange Glazed Carrots
Made with Moravian Spice Cookie Streusel Topping

For the Streusel Topping
Place all ingredients except melted butter in a mixing bowl and toss to combine. Drizzle butter over mix and toss to coat and distribute. Season with a pinch of salt.

For the Carrots
Toss all the ingredients in a large shallow casserole dish and top with topping. Bake in 350° oven 35-45 minutes until golden brown.

For the Plating
Place a large spoonful alongside roast turkey, glazed ham or pork.

Ingredients

For the Streusel Topping
1/2 c. hazelnuts, finely chopped
1/2 c. pecans, finely chopped
1/2 c. Moravian Spice Cookie Crumbles
1/4 c. granola
1/4 c. brown sugar
2 tsp. cinnamon
1 stick (4 oz.) melted unsalted butter
pinch salt

For the Carrots
juice & zest from 3 oranges
3 tbsp. honey
1 tsp. ground cinnamon
pinch ground cloves
1 tsp. salt
3 lbs. carrots, peeled & sliced at a 45° angle, 1/2" thick

Sweet Potato-Crab Fritters
Made with Lemon Caper Remoulade

For the Sauce
Combine all ingredients in a mixing bowl and mix thoroughly.

For the Fritters
Combine all ingredients except for cookies, crackers and lump crab. Mix thoroughly. Add the crackers and cookies and mix. Add the lump crab and fold in gently. Allow to rest 8-10 minutes for the starch to absorb the liquid. Using a 1/2 oz. scoop, scoop the batter into a 375° deep fryer and fry 4-8 minutes until fritters float and are cooked through.

For the Plating
Serve the fritters on a plate lined with paper towels. Serve the sauce in a cup on the side. These are perfect as an appetizer.

Ingredients

For the Sauce
1/2 c. mayonnaise
grated zest & juice of 1 lemon
1 tbsp. Dijon mustard
1 tbsp. capers
1 tbsp. pickle, diced finely
1/2 sm shallot, diced finely
dash of pickle juice
dash of hot sauce
pinch fresh parsley, chopped
salt & pepper

For the Fritters
1/2 c. mayonnaise
2 eggs, beaten
2 c. sweet potatoes, peeled & grated
1 bunch scallions, sliced thin
1/2 rib celery, diced finely
1/2 red bell pepper, diced finely
1/2 c. corn, freshly cut
1/2 c. saltine crackers, crushed
1/2 c. Moravian Lemon Cookie Crumbles
1 lb. lump crabmeat

Crab Fritters

Brie En Croute

Made with Granny Smith Apples, Smoked Ham & Moravian Spice Cookies

For the Brie

Thaw puff pastry in refrigerator overnight. Scrape the bloom off Brie rind with a sharp knife. Place the brie on top of the puff pastry and cut a square with a 3-inch overhang. Wrap the puff pastry around the Brie starting with a corner by pulling it inward toward the center of the wheel. Follow with the next corner of dough, folding it over and making a crease. Repeat until Brie is wrapped completely. Place Brie on a greased sheet pan and brush pastry with the egg yolk and milk beaten together. Bake at 375° for 18-25 minutes or until crust has risen and is well browned.

For the Plating

Cut the Brie into wedges. Serve on a plate with thinly sliced smoked ham, sliced Granny Smith apples and Moravian Spice Cookies.

Ingredients

For the Brie
1 sheet puff pastry
1 lrg Brie wheel, 24-32 oz.
1 egg yolk
2 tbsp. milk

For the Plating
smoked ham
Granny Smith apples, sliced & dressed
    with lemon juice
Moravian Spice Cookies

Brie En Croute

Spinach & Arugula Salad

Made with Moravian Spice Cookie Crusted Goat Cheese Cake, D'Anjou Pears, Honey Roasted Peanuts & Raspberry Balsamic Vinaigrette

For the Vinaigrette
Place vinegar, raspberries, and sugar in a medium saucepan and bring to a simmer. Allow to simmer for 5-6 minutes so that the raspberries begin to break down. Stir with a whisk to help break apart raspberries, leaving some small pieces in the mixture for presentation. Remove from heat and place mixture in plastic bowl uncovered. Place in refrigerator to cool. Once cool, cover and reserve. Can be made one week in advance.

For the Goat Cheese Cakes
Chill the goat cheese well. Form four small patties with the cheese (a thinner patty gives a better crust-to-cheese ratio) and chill again. This can be done one day in advance. When ready to serve the salads, place the cookie crumbs in a bowl and press the goat cheese cakes in firmly to encrust them with the crumbs. Present on top of dressed salad.

For the Salad
Wash and trim the arugula and spinach. Slice the pear by cutting straight down about a 1/4 inch from the core. Make a 90 degree turn as if cutting a square around the core. Lay cut pieces flat side down and slice thin slices from the sections. Set aside. Place greens in a large mixing bowl, drizzling with a little extra virgin olive oil and tossing to coat. Season with kosher salt and fresh ground black pepper. Set aside.

For the Plating
Take a spoonful of the vinaigrette and pour a 2" pool close to the rim of the plate (white plates make a nice contrast to the colors). Drag your spoon through the pool across the plate. Place the dressed greens on the end of the smear. Top with peanuts and pear slices. Finish with the goat cheese cakes propped against the salad.

Find the Goat Cheese Cakes Addictive?
Try them for an exotic twist on dessert with warm chocolate sauce, fresh raspberries and whipped cream.

Ingredients

For the Vinaigrette
1/2 c. balsamic vinegar
1/2 c. frozen raspberries
3 tsp. sugar

For the Goat Cheese Cakes
12 oz. fresh goat milk cheese
1 c. Moravian Spice Cookie Crumbles

For the Salad
8 oz. arugula
12 oz. baby spinach
1 D'Anjou pear
extra virgin olive oil
Kosher salt & pepper
4 oz. honey roasted peanuts

Boston Lettuce Salad

Made with Balsamic Vinaigrette, Toasted Almonds, Chopped Egg, Bacon, Red Onion & Moravian Spice Cookie Crusted Bleu Cheese Croutons

For the Dressing
Whisk together all the ingredients except the oil in a bowl. Slowly drizzle the oil in as you quickly whisk to incorporate the oil. Season with salt and pepper to taste.

For the Salad
Pull the leaves off the head, leaving them whole. Toss the leaves in a large bowl with the vinaigrette. Stack the leaves in bowls and top with other ingredients.

For the Croutons
Mix the egg and milk together. Dredge the cheese in flour, dip in egg-milk mixture and finish by breading with cookie crumbles. Deep fry in 350° oil for 3-5 minutes.

For the Plating
Garnish the salad with the fried croutons.

Ingredients

For the Dressing
1/4 c. balsamic vinegar
2 tbsp. Dijon mustard
1 tsp. minced shallot
1 tsp. honey
1 c. extra virgin olive oil
salt & pepper

For the Salad
2 heads Boston lettuce
4 oz. toasted almond slices
2 hard-boiled eggs, chopped
8 oz. crispy bacon, chopped
1/2 red onion, thinly sliced
1/2 c. grape tomatoes, sliced in half

For the Croutons
8 oz. bleu cheese wedge, 1/2" cubed
1 c. flour
2 eggs
1/2 c. milk
2 c. Moravian Spice Cookie Crumbles

Summer Sausage Canapés

Made with Moravian Orange-Cranberry Cookie, Grain Mustard & Summer Sausage

For the Canapés
Top each cookie with a slice of the sausage, a dollop of the mustard and a slice of the cornichons.

For the Plating
Serve on a platter with more of the sliced sausage, mustard, cornichons and aged cheddar.

Ingredients

Moravian Orange-Cranberry Cookies
sliced summer sausage
grain mustard
cornichons, sliced

Summer Sausage Canapes

Moravian Lemon Cookie Canapés
Made with Chicken-Grape-Walnut Salad

For the Canapés
Combine chicken, mayonnaise, celery and dill. Add walnuts, apple and grapes. Mix. Add more mayonnaise to taste.

For the Plating
Place Moravian Lemon Cookies on a large platter. Top each with a dollop of chicken salad mix.

Ingredients

1 roasted chicken, skinned & picked
   (approx. 3 - 4 cups)
1/2 c. mayonnaise
1 rib celery, diced finely
1 tbsp. fresh dill, chopped
1/4 c. walnut pieces
1/4 Granny Smith apple, diced
1/2 c. grapes, halved
One 4.75 oz. tube Moravian Lemon
   Cookies

Chicken Salad Canapes

Cold Flemish Buttermilk & Apple Soup
Made with Moravian Spice Cookies

For the Soup
Combine the buttermilk, sugar and applesauce in a large mixing bowl. Peel and grate apples into the soup mixture. Stir well. Chill in refrigerator for 30 minutes to allow the flavor to develop.

For the Plating
Ladle soup into bowls. Top with sliced apples and Moravian Spice Cookie Crumbles for garnish.

The Flemish Are Coming
Flemish describes a portion of the people of Belgium, the same people who brought us some of the finest foods of our time: french fries, waffles, waterzooie, and some of the world's finest beers.

What Is an Intermezzo?
Intermezzos are small servings between courses, usually between dinner and dessert. They are designed to cleanse your palette of any lingering aftertastes.

Ingredients

For the Soup
1/2 gal. buttermilk
1/2 c. confectioners sugar
2 c. prepared applesauce
4 Granny Smith apples, peeled & grated
1/4 c. Moravian Spice Cookie Crumbles

Feta Cheese Skewers

Made with Extra Virgin Olive Oil, Basil, Lemon & Moravian Lemon Cookie Crumbles

For the Skewers
Skewer a basil leaf and then a cube of feta cheese. Repeat until all cheese is skewered. Place skewers on their side on a large platter. Drizzle with extra virgin olive oil, lemon juice, zest and Moravian Lemon Cookie Crumbles.

For the Plating
Serve the skewers on a large platter with sliced Italian meats such as salami, prosciutto and cappicola.

Ingredients

For the Skewers
30 sm basil leaves
One 8 oz. block feta cheese, cut into
 1/4" cubes
2 tbsp. extra virgin olive oil
zest & juice of 1 lemon
1/4 c. Moravian Lemon Cookie
 Crumbles

For the Plating
assorted sliced Italian meats (salami,
 prosciutto, cappicola)

Moravian Pumpkin Spice Cookie Canapés

With Prosciutto-Wrapped Green Apple

For the Canapés
Place cookies on a tray and top with green apple wedges wrapped in a small piece of prosciutto.

For the Plating
Serve on a platter with some of the other Moravian Cookie canapés.

Ingredients

For the Canapés
One 4.75 oz. tube Moravian Pumpkin Spice Cookies
2 Granny Smith apples, peeled, cored & cut into wedges, tossed in lemon juice
6 oz. prosciutto, thinly sliced

Pumpkin Spice Canapes

Moravian Spice Cookie Canapés

Made with Kasseri Cheese, Sweet Onions, Roasted Tomatoes & Oregano

For the Canapés

Sweat the onion in a sautépan in olive oil over medium heat until translucent and tender (15-20 minutes). Season with salt and pepper. Toss the cherry tomatoes with olive oil, salt and pepper. Roast in oven at 425° for 5-8 minutes until tender. Top the Moravian Spice Cookies with triangular slices of the Kasseri cheese, topped with a few of the onions, a roasted tomato half and a sprinkle of fresh oregano.

For the Plating

Serve canapés on a large platter with lemon-basil marinated artichokes and pickled mushrooms.

About Kasseri Cheese

Kasseri is a sharp sheep's milk cheese that comes from Greece. This canapé is a takeoff on a classic Greek dish, a flaming tomato casserole called saganaki: fresh sliced tomatoes layered with fresh garlic, sweated onions, oregano, feta cheese and Kasseri cheese.

Ingredients

For the Canapés

1 lrg yellow onion, diced small
olive oil
salt & pepper
24 cherry tomatoes, halved
One 4.75 oz. tube Moravian Spice
   Cookies
8 oz. Kasseri cheese
2 tbsp. fresh oregano, chopped

For the Plating

lemon-basil marinated artichokes
pickled mushrooms

Kasseri Canapes

Ultimate Mac & Cheese Bake
Made with Moravian Spice Cookie Crumbles Topping

For the Cheese Sauce
In a large saucepan over medium heat, melt the butter, add the flour and cook 3-5 minutes until slightly toasted. Add the milk bit by bit, whisking vigorously until the first addition is completely incorporated before adding the next. Once all the milk has been added, simmer the sauce for 10-15 minutes to thicken slightly and season with fresh grated nutmeg, salt, and pepper. Remove the sauce from the heat and finish the sauce by adding the cheese (use only 1/4 cup of the Parmigiano and reserve the rest for topping) bit by bit and whisking to incorporate. Once all cheese is added, whisk in the beaten eggs.

For the Mac & Cheese
Toss the pasta and cheese sauce in a large deep casserole dish. In a separate mixing bowl mix the bread crumbs, cookie crumbles, butter, parsley, garlic powder, and remaining Parmigiano and top the casserole with the crumb topping. Cover with foil and bake in a 350° oven for 45-60 minutes until set and macaroni is cooked, then remove the foil and place the oven on broil and brown the topping 4-6 minutes.

For the Plating
This is a great dish for family reunions, potlucks or holiday spreads. It goes well with roast chicken, glazed ham alongside turnips or collard greens.

Ingredients

For the Cheese Sauce
1/2 lb. unsalted butter
1/2 lb. flour
1/2 gal. milk
fresh nutmeg, grated
salt & pepper
1/2 c. shredded Provolone
1/2 c. shredded sharp cheddar
1/4 c. shredded Asiago
1/2 c. shredded Parmigiano, divided
3 eggs, beaten well

For the Mac & Cheese
2 lb. elbow macaroni, gemelli or
    cavatappi, uncooked
cheese sauce (above)
1 c. Italian bread crumbs
1/2 c. Moravian Spice Cookie
    Crumbles
2 tbsp. unsalted butter, melted
2 tbsp. fresh flat-leaf parsley, chopped
pinch garlic powder

Baked Sweet Potato

Made with Orange-Honey Butter & Moravian Spice Cookie Crumbles

For the Sweet Potatoes

Preheat oven to 400°. Bake sweet potatoes until you can insert the prongs of a fork with little effort. This can take anywhere from 45 minutes to an hour, depending on the size of the sweet potato. While potatoes are baking, beat the marmalade, honey and butter in a large bowl. Season lightly with salt. Cut potatoes lengthwise without completely splitting them open. Drop a spoonful of the butter mixture into each potato and finish with crushed cookies. Serve remaining butter and cookie crumbs on the side for customization.

Ingredients

4 lrg sweet potatoes
2 tbsp. orange marmalade
2 tsp. honey
4 oz. unsalted butter,
    room temperature
salt
1/2 c. Moravian Spice Cookies,
crushed

Roasted Root Vegetable Cobbler

For the Topping

Combine all the ingredients in a mixing bowl and toss.

For the Cobbler

Combine all ingredients in a large baking dish. Season with salt and pepper. Roast in oven at 400° for 30-45 minutes until vegetables are roasted and tender and liquid is reduced to a glaze. Toss vegetables to coat in the glaze. Place in a smaller casserole dish, press down flat, top with crumb topping and return to the oven at 350° for 15-20 minutes until topping is browned.

For the Plating

Scoop out a serving of the vegetables with the topping onto a plate.

Ingredients

For the Topping
1/2 c. Moravian Orange-Cranberry
 Cookies
2 oz. melted unsalted butter
1/2 c. granola
1/4 c. brown sugar
1/4 c. pecans, chopped
1/4 c. almonds, chopped
pinch salt

For the Cobbler
1 med butternut squash, peeled
 & 1/2 cubed
1 lrg sweet potato, peeled
 & 1/2 cubed
2 lrg parsnips, peeled & thick
 sliced on a bias
2 lrg carrots, peeled & thick
 sliced on a bias
1 med rutabaga, peeled
 & 1/2 cubed
2 med turnips, peeled & 1/2 cubed
1 c. apple cider
One 14-oz. can chicken broth
salt & pepper

Vegetable Cobbler

Broccoli Cheddar Bacon Casserole
Made with Moravian Spice Cookie Crumble Topping

For the Casserole Base
In a large saucepan, melt the butter over medium heat and sweat the onions and garlic until translucent. Add the flour and cook the mixture, whisking often for 3-5 minutes until slightly darker. Then begin adding the milk in gradually, whisking in the first addition completely before adding the next. Once all the liquid has been added, simmer the sauce on medium-low for 5-7 minutes until thickened. Remove the sauce from heat and finish with the herbs and whisk in the cheese last, bit by bit, and season to taste with salt and pepper. Place the bacon and broccoli in a large deep casserole dish, pour the sauce over the top of the broccoli and toss to coat.

For the Crumb Topping
Combine all ingredients and spread over the top of the casserole. Cover with foil and bake in 375° oven for 35-45 minutes. Remove foil, switch oven to broil and continue to bake 3-5 minutes until golden brown.

For the Plating
Serve a generous spoonful alongside roast chicken, turkey or pork.

Ingredients

For the Casserole Base
4 oz. unsalted butter
1 sm yellow onion, diced small
1 clove garlic, minced
4 oz. flour
4 c. milk
1 tbsp. fresh flat-leaf parsley, chopped
1/2 c. shredded sharp cheddar
salt & pepper
4 oz. cooked bacon, chopped
3 lbs. broccoli

For the Crumb Topping
1 oz. unsalted butter, melted
1 c. Italian bread crumbs seasoned
1/4 c. Moravian Spice Cookie
  Crumbles
1/4 c. shredded Parmigiano
1/4 c. shredded sharp cheddar

Spaghetti Squash Casserole

For the Casserole
Cut the squash in half lengthwise and place in a large baking dish with 1/4 inch of water. Cover and roast in oven at 400° for 30-45 minutes until squash is tender and flakes easily with a fork. Scrape the squash with a fork to break the pulp up into strings. While the squash is roasting, bring the cream to a simmer with the cranberries and brie. Add the squash strings to the cream and season with salt and pepper. Place in a shallow baking dish, top with Moravian Cranberry-Orange Cookie Crumbles and bake at 400° for 10-15 minutes until lightly browned on top.

For the Plating
Serve a generous scoop alongside poultry or pork.

Ingredients

1 large spaghetti squash, halved with
  seeds removed
1 1/2 c. heavy cream
1/4 c. dried cranberries
4 oz. brie cheese (rind removed)
salt & pepper
1/4 c. Moravian Cranberry-Orange
  Cookie Crumbles

Squash Casserole
Made with Moravian Spice Cookie Crumble Topping

For the Casserole Base
In a large saucepan, melt the butter over medium heat. Sweat the onions and garlic until translucent. Add the flour and cook the mixture, whisking often for 3-5 minutes until slightly darker. Begin adding the milk in little by little, whisking in the first addition completely before adding the next. Once all the liquid has been added, allow the sauce to simmer on medium low for 5-7 minutes until thickened. Remove the sauce from the heat. Finish with the herbs. Whisk in the cheese last, bit by bit. Season to taste with salt and pepper. Slice the squash 1/4" thick and place in a large deep casserole dish. Pour the sauce over the top of the squash and toss to coat.

For the Crumb Topping
Combine all ingredients and spread over the top of the casserole. Cover with foil and bake at 375° for 35-45 minutes. Remove foil and turn oven to broil. Continue to bake for 3-5 minutes until golden brown.

For the Plating
Serve a generous spoonful of casserole alongside roast chicken, turkey or pork.

Ingredients

For the Casserole Base
4 oz. unsalted butter
1 sm yellow onion, diced small
1 clove garlic, minced
4 oz. flour
4 c. milk
2 tsp. fresh thyme, chopped
1 tsp. fresh sage, chopped
1/2 c. sharp white cheddar, shredded
salt & pepper
3 lbs. assorted soft yellow squash,
    zucchini, patty pan & zephyr

For the Crumb Topping
1 oz. unsalted butter, melted
1 c. Italian seasoned bread crumbs
1/4 c. Moravian Spice Cookie
    Crumbles
1/4 c. shredded Parmigiano
1/4 c. shredded sharp white cheddar
1 tbsp. fresh flat-leaf parsley, chopped
salt & pepper

Green Bean Casserole
Made with Moravian Spice Cookie Crumbles Topping

For the Casserole Base
In a large saucepan, melt the butter over medium heat and sweat the onions, mushrooms and garlic until translucent. Add the flour and cook the mixture, whisking often for 3-5 minutes until slightly darker. Begin adding the liquids in little by little, whisking in the first addition completely before adding the next. Once all the liquid has been added, allow the sauce to simmer on medium-low for 5-7 minutes until thickened. Remove the sauce from the heat and finish with the herbs. Whisk in the cheese last, bit by bit. Season to taste with salt and pepper. Place the green beans in a large deep casserole dish, pour the sauce over the top of the green beans and toss to coat.

For the Crumb Topping
Combine all ingredients. Spread over the top of the casserole. Cover with foil and bake at 375° for 35-45 minutes. Remove foil and turn oven to broil. Continue to bake 3-5 minutes until golden brown.

For the Plating
Serve a generous spoonful along side roast chicken, turkey or pork.

Ingredients

For the Casserole Base
4 oz. unsalted butter
1 sm yellow onion, diced small
8 oz. mushrooms, sliced
1 clove garlic, minced
4 oz. flour
2 c. beef broth
2 c. heavy cream
2 tsp. fresh thyme, chopped
1 tsp. fresh sage, chopped
1/2 c. shredded sharp cheddar
salt & pepper
3 lbs. green beans

For the Crumb Topping
1 oz. unsalted butter, melted
1 c. Italian seasoned breadcrumbs
1/4 c. Moravian Spice Cookie
   Crumbles
1/4 c. shredded Parmigiano
1/4 c. shredded sharp cheddar
1 tbsp. fresh flat-leaf parsley, chopped
salt & pepper

Crispy Moravian Tangerine Orange Cookie Crusted Chicken

Made with Orange Sesame Glaze

For the Sauce
Combine all ingredients except cilantro in a saucepan. Bring to a simmer for 10-15 minutes. Finish with the cilantro and set aside. Can be made one week in advance.

For the Chicken
In a large mixing bowl, combine flour and water to make a paste. Add the chicken and toss to coat with the flour-water paste. Season with salt and pepper. Toss in another mixing bowl with Moravian Tangerine Orange Cookie Crumbles. Fry in a deep fryer at 350° for 8-9 minutes. Once cooked through, toss chicken in sauce. Garnish with toasted sesame seeds and fresh chopped cilantro.

For the Plating
Serve the crispy chicken tossed in the sauce over jasmine rice with a stir fry of broccoli, scallion, shiitake mushrooms and cashews.

Ingredients

For the Sauce
1/2 c. Stubbs Spicy Barbecue Sauce
1/2 c. orange marmalade
2 tbsp. toasted sesame seeds
1 tbsp. fresh ginger, chopped
1 tbsp. fresh cilantro, chopped

For the Chicken
Three 8 oz. chicken breasts, cut into thin strips
1/2 c. water
1/2 c. flour
3 c. Moravian Tangerine Orange Cookie Crumbles
salt & pepper

For the Plating
Jasmine rice
stir fried broccoli, scallion, shitake mushrooms and cashews

Tangerine Crusted Chicken

Herb Roasted Chicken
Made with Chestnut & Moravian Spice Cookie Stuffing with Herb Roasting Jus

For the Stuffing
Sweat the vegetables with butter in a sautépan over medium heat until translucent. Add the chestnuts, giblets and herbs. Sauté for an additional 2-3 minutes. Prepare the dressing according to directions, using the chicken broth. Add the vegetable mixture to the stuffing. Mix with Moravian Spice Cookie Crumbles. Bake at 350° for 30-45 minutes.

For the Chicken
Wrap the garlic in foil and bake at 375° for 30-40 minutes until roasted and very soft. While the garlic is roasting ,wash the chicken and pat dry. Season chicken with salt and pepper. Place in a deep roasting pan and bake at 400° for 45-60 minutes. For the basting liquid, add the chopped herbs to the butter and squeeze 3-4 cloves of the roasted garlic into a saucepan. Melt over medium heat for 5-6 minutes until butter is aromatic and melted. Baste the chicken with the butter every 5-7 minutes throughout the cooking process.

For the Roasting Jus
While the chicken rests, place the pan the chicken was roasted in on the range on medium heat. Add the roasted garlic and vegetables and sauté for 4-6 minutes until softened. Deglaze the pan with the chicken broth and simmer for 10-15 minutes until jus is reduced slightly. Finish with the herbs and simmer an additional 3-5 minutes before straining the jus into a gravy boat.

For the Plating
To carve the chicken, cut off the wings and leg quarters and separate the leg from the thigh. Cut the breasts off of the bone. Scoop some of the stuffing onto a plate. Slice some of the breast meat and place either a leg, thigh or wing on the plate. Sauce with roasting jus.

Sot-l'y-laisse
Sot-l'y-laisse is the French term for what we call the oyster of the chicken. Once the bird is roasted, flip it over. Right above the hip are two round recesses that hold the richest most flavorful pieces of meat on the bird, usually the bounty of the carver.

Ingredients

For the Stuffing
1 small yellow onion, diced small
1 stalk celery, diced small
1 parsnip, peeled & diced small
5 fresh chestnuts roasted, peeled & chopped or 1 can chestnuts, chopped
chicken giblets, diced small & sautéed (optional)
2 tsp. fresh sage, chopped
2 tsp. fresh thyme, chopped
2 tsp. fresh rosemary, chopped
One 16 oz. package stuffing mix
One 14 oz. can chicken broth
1/2 c. Moravian Spice Cookie Crumbles

For the Chicken
1 head garlic
One 3 1/2 - 4 lbs chicken
2 tbsp. fresh flat-leaf parsley, chopped
1 tbsp. fresh rosemary, chopped
1 tbsp. fresh thyme, chopped
1 tbsp. fresh sage, chopped
1/2 c. butter, melted
salt & pepper

For the Roasting Jus
1/2 head roasted garlic
1/2 stalk celery, diced small
1/2 small onion, diced small
1/2 carrot, peeled & diced small
1 parsnip, peeled & diced small
2 cans chicken broth
herbs from the basting liquid

Herb Roasted Chicken

Banana Pudding
With Moravian Vanilla Walnut Cookies

For the Pudding
Make the pudding with the milk according to the directions. Allow to set in the refrigerator. Once set, fold in the whipped topping and mashed bananas. Place a layer of Moravian Vanilla Walnut Cookies on the bottom of a deep glass bowl and top with some of the pudding. Repeat the layers until remaining pudding is used.

For the Plating
Serve a generous spoonful in a bowl with extra whipped topping and more of the cookies.

Ingredients

2 lrg packets banana pudding
4 c. milk
1 lrg container whipped topping
6 very ripe bananas
1 lrg tube Moravian Vanilla Walnut Cookies

Stewed Apples & Pears

Made with Vanilla Ice Cream & Moravian Spice Cookies

For the Apples & Pears

Melt butter in a saucepan over medium heat and add brown sugar. Cook until slightly bubbly. Add apples, pears, cloves and cinnamon. Stir. Allow to simmer 4-8 minutes and remove from heat. Allow to cool slightly before serving.

For the Plating

Place two scoops of vanilla ice cream in a bowl. Spoon some of the stewed fruits over ice cream. Garnish with Moravian Spice Cookies.

It's Peach Season

This dish works very well with peaches. Select four to six large ripe peaches, peeled and sliced into wedges. Use the same recipe, omitting the cinnamon and clove. Substitute 2 oz. peach schnapps instead.

Ingredients

2 Granny Smith apples, peeled & cut into wedges
2 D'Anjou pears, peeled & cut into wedges
1/2 c. brown sugar
1/2 stick unsalted butter
2 tsp. ground cinnamon
pinch ground cloves
Moravian Spice Cookies

Moravian Cranberry Orange Cookie Crusted Pork Cutlet
Made with Cornbread-Sausage–Apple-Spice Cookie Stuffing & Apple Mango Chutney

For the Stuffing
In a large skillet over medium heat, break up sausage into large crumbles and fry until cooked. Remove sausage, using a slotted spoon and place on a paper-lined plate to drain. Use some of the sausage grease to fry the onions, celery and apples. Cook until apples are soft and onions translucent. Add the herbs and season with salt and pepper. Add the sautéed mixture and chicken broth to the spice cookies and cornbread stuffing mix. Bake according to the stuffing directions. Reserve warm.

For the Chutney
Bring the vinegar and sugar to a boil. Reduce to simmer. Allow to simmer 4-5 minutes. Add the mango and apple. Allow to simmer an additional 4-5 minutes. Finish with the sweet chili sauce. Reserve. Best served slightly warm, but not hot. This can be made one week in advance.

For the Cutlets
Season the cutlets with salt and pepper. Dredge in flour, dip in egg-milk mixture and finish by breading with Moravian Cranberry Orange Cookie Crumbles. Place on a lightly greased, foil-lined cookie sheet and bake at 400° for 4-5 minutes. Flip and finish cooking another 4-5 minutes. Reserve warm.

For the Plating
Place spoonful of stuffing mix on plate. Lean pork cutlets against stuffing mix. Drizzle sauce around the plate.

On Making Friends with the Butcher
Butcher shops or meat markets are almost a thing of the past. If you are lucky enough to have one in your city or neighborhood, please frequent it to help preserve this fading trade. The meats are almost always higher quality, and special requests like pounding cutlets or custom cutting the choicest steaks are met with a smile. Even if you are not fortunate enough to have a butcher near you, get to know the staff at the meat counter in your grocery store. Remember to take care of them, whether it be with gratuities or Moravian Cookies.

Like the Chutney?
Chutney makes a great addition to turkey or chicken salad sandwiches with lettuce, tomato and brie cheese on a crusty roll, croissant or in a wrap.

Ingredients

For the Stuffing
1 lb. fresh country style sausage
1 rib celery, diced small
1 sm yellow onion, diced small
2 Granny Smith apples, diced
1/2 tbsp. fresh sage, chopped
1/2 tbsp. fresh rosemary, chopped
1 tsp. fresh thyme, chopped
1/2 c. Moravian Spice Cookies
1 package cornbread stuffing mix
1 can chicken broth (may use more, depending on stuffing mix)
salt & pepper

For the Chutney
1/2 c. cider vinegar
1/2 c. sugar
2 Granny Smith apples, diced
1 lrg mango, slightly firm, peeled & diced
3 tsp. Asian/Thai sweet chili sauce

For the Cutlets
8 sm pork cutlets
1 c. flour
2 eggs
1/2 c. milk
2 c. Moravian Cranberry Orange Cookie Crumbles
salt & pepper

Pork Cutlet

Crispy Moravian Lemon Cookie Crusted Crab Cakes
With Tartar Sauce

For the Tartar Sauce
Combine all ingredients in a mixing bowl and season to taste.

For the Crab Cakes
Begin by sweating the vegetables in the butter in a sautépan until trans-lucent and aromatic. Add the seasoning and remove from the heat. Trans-fer to a bowl and allow to cool in the refrigerator. Mix the mayonnaise, egg, mustard and lemon together in a mixing bowl. Add the chilled sau-téed vegetables and incorporate. Open the crabmeat and examine for any shell fragments (careful not to break up the big lumps). Keep the Backfin crabmeat separate from other crab. Season with salt and pepper. Add the crushed Ritz Crackers to the mayonnaise mix, tossing to incorporate. Add the backfin crab, tossing to incorporate. Add the jumbo lump crab last, being careful to toss just enough to incorporate it into the mix. Place covered mix in refrigerator and allow to rest for 15-20 minutes. This allows the crackers to absorb the liquid component of the mix and to thicken enough to make the cakes. Once chilled, form into 1" thick by 3" wide patties. Lightly dredge in Moravian Lemon Cookie Crumbles. Fry patties in butter in a sautépan on medium heat until lightly golden brown (3-4 minutes). Flip to brown the other side. Finish in oven at 375° oven for 7-9 minutes.

For the Plating
Place a spoonful of the tartar sauce on the plate and smooth it over with the back of a spoon. Place two of the crabcakes–one shingled on top of the other–toward the end of the sauce smear. Serve with a salad of greens tossed with vinaigrette or slaw and corn on the cob.

Crabs Love Mayonnaise & Butter
Crabmeat is very lean and therefore craves a little extra fat to bring out its natural flavors. It especially craves mayonnaise and butter.

On Buying Crabmeat
Crabmeat is sold in many types. For this recipe, you can use the pasteur-ized canned crabmeat found in the seafood section of your grocery store. Use 1/2 special crabmeat to aid in the binding of the crab cakes and to reduce cost. Then finish with jumbo lump for presentation.

Ingredients

For the Tartar Sauce
1/2 c. mayonnaise
1 tbsp. Dijon mustard
1 kosher dill pickle, minced fine
1 tbsp. red onion, minced fine
1 tbsp. kosher pickle juice
1 tbsp. pickled cherry peppers, minced fine
1 hard-boiled egg, chopped
1 tsp. capers
pinch fresh dill, chopped
pinch fresh flat-leaf parsley, chopped
pinch sugar
salt & pepper

For the Crab Cakes
2 tbsp. unsalted butter
1/2 rib celery, minced
2 tbsp. yellow onion, diced fine
4 scallions, green & whites sliced thin
1 tsp. red bell pepper, diced fine
dash hot sauce
1/2 tsp. Old Bay seasoning
1/2 c. mayonnaise
1 egg
1 tbsp. Dijon mustard
juice of 1/2 lemon
12-14 Ritz crackers, crushed
salt & pepper
2 lb. can crabmeat (1 lb. jumbo lump & 1 lb. special or backfin recommended)
2 c. Moravian Lemon Cookie Crumbles

For the Plating
green salad, tossed with vinaigrette
slaw
corn on the cob

Crab Cakes

Spinach Gratin
Made with Moravian Spice Cookie Crumbles Topping

For the Gratin Base
In a large saucepan, melt the butter over medium heat. Sweat the onions and garlic until translucent. Add the flour and cook the mixture, whisking often for 3-5 minutes until slightly darker. Begin adding the cream in little by little, whisking in the first addition completely before adding the next. Once all the liquid has been added, allow the sauce to simmer on medium low for 5-7 minutes until thickened. Remove the sauce from the heat. Finish with the herbs. Whisk in the cheese last, bit by bit. Season to taste with salt and pepper. Place the spinach in a large shallow casserole dish. Pour the sauce over the top of the spinach and toss to coat.

For the Crumb Topping
Combine all ingredients and spread over the top of the casserole. Cover with foil and bake at 375° for 35-45 minutes. Remove foil and turn oven to broil. Continue to bake for 3-5 minutes until golden brown.

For the Plating
Serve a generous spoonful alongside roast chicken, turkey or grilled steaks.

Ingredients

For the Gratin Base
4 oz. unsalted butter
1 small yellow onion, diced small
1 clove garlic, minced
4 oz. flour
4 c. heavy cream
2 tsp. fresh thyme, chopped
1 tsp. fresh sage, chopped
1/2 c. shredded sharp white cheddar
salt & pepper
3 lbs. baby spinach, blanched & squeezed dry

For the Crumb Topping
1 oz. unsalted butter, melted
1 c. Italian seasoned bread crumbs
1/4 c. Moravian Spice Cookie Crumbles
1/4 c. shredded Parmigiano
1/4 c. shredded sharp white cheddar
1 tbsp. fresh flat-leaf parsley, chopped
salt & pepper

Tomatoes Gratin

Made with Moravian Lemon Cookie Crumb Topping

For the Tomatoes

Toss the tomatoes, scallions, garlic and herbs together in a mixing bowl. Season with the salt, pepper and olive oil. Pour mix into large shallow casserole dish. Sprinkle the cheeses over the top of the casserole.

For the Crumb Topping

Combine all ingredients and spread over the top of the casserole. Cover with foil and bake at 375° for 20-25 minutes. Remove foil and turn oven to broil. Continue to bake 3-5 minutes until golden brown.

Ingredients

For the Tomatoes
3 lbs. ripe mixed medium tomatoes, chopped & sliced
1 clove garlic, minced
1 bunch scallions, sliced
1 tbsp. fresh oregano, chopped
1 tbsp. fresh basil, chopped
olive oil
salt & pepper
1/2 c. feta cheese crumbles
1 1/2 c. shredded Kasseri cheese
1/2 c. shredded Asiago

For the Crumb Topping
1 oz. unsalted butter, melted
1 c. Italian seasoned bread crumbs
1/4 c. Moravian Lemon Cookie Crumbles
1/4 c. shredded Parmigiano
1/4 c. shredded Kasseri cheese
1 tbsp. fresh flat-leaf parsley, chopped
salt & pepper

Asparagus Gratin

Made with Brie, White Wine & Moravian Spice Cookies

For the Asparagus

In a saucepan, melt butter and sweat shallots over medium heat until shallots are translucent (2-4 minutes). Add flour to make a roux and cook an additional 5 minutes to lightly toast the roux. Deglaze with the white wine and whisk vigorously. Add cream bit by bit, whisking constantly and allowing the first addition of liquid to be absorbed before adding more. Once the sauce is thickened, whisk in the brie. Season with salt and pepper.

For the Gratin

Sauté the mushrooms on medium high with butter until lightly browned (8-10 minutes). Trim the ends of the asparagus and spread in a shallow baking dish. Top with the sautéed mushrooms and gratin base. Then top with the Asiago cheese and cookie crumbles. Bake at 375° for 15-18 minutes, until asparagus is tender and topping is browned.

For the Plating

Scoop out some of the casserole along with the sauce and mushrooms.

Ingredients

For the Asparagus
2 tbsp. unsalted butter
2 sm shallots, diced
2 tbsp. flour
1/2 c. dry white wine
2 c. heavy cream
4 oz. brie cheese
salt & pepper

For the Gratin
1 bunch pencil asparagus
8 lrg button mushrooms, sliced
gratin base (above)
1/8 c. grated Asiago cheese
1/4 c. Moravian Spice Cookie
 Crumbles

Asparagus Gratin

Hazelnut Freezer Pie

Made with Moravian Double Chocolate Cookie Crust

For the Crust
Combine all ingredients in a mixing bowl and toss. Mixture should look like wet sand. Press down into a pie plate to make the crust. Refrigerate.

For the Filling
Beat Nutella with mixer until loose. Fold in whipped topping, using a spatula until light and fluffy. Fold in hazelnuts. Pour mixture into refrigerated piecrust. Place in freezer for at least 3 1/2 hours to allow to set up. Remove pie 30-45 minutes before serving.

For the Plating
Cut pie into 10 slices. Serve with a light drizzle of hot fudge ice cream topping, chopped toasted hazelnuts, whipped topping and fresh strawberries or raspberries.

On Nutella
Nutella is the Canadian answer to peanut butter, a rich and creamy spread of hazelnuts. Very chocolaty in taste, the spread works well with sweets. Try the spread on the Moravian cookies with a glass of milk.

Ingredients

For the Crust
1 1/2 c. Moravian Double Chocolate Cookie Crumbles
6 oz. (1 1/2 sticks) unsalted butter, melted
pinch salt

For the Filling
3 jars Nutella
3 med container whipped topping
1 1/2 c. hazelnuts, chopped

Hazelnut Freezer Pie

Florentines

Italian Chocolate Dipped Cookies

For the Cookies

Mix nuts and fruits in a mixing bowl. Reserve. In a double boiler, melt chocolate in a mixing bowl, stirring constantly until completely melted and smooth. Remove from heat and continue to stir for 8-10 minutes until slightly cooler. Dip cookies in chocolate halfway and coat chocolate with fruit and nut mixture. Lay cookies out on wax paper and allow to dry and cool completely before packing in tins.

Easy Homemade Gifts

These make a great homemade gift for the holiday season and are a fun project to get the little ones involved in. What kid doesn't get excited at the sight of melted chocolate dripping from cookies?

Ingredients

1 tube Moravian Double Chocolate Cookies
1 tube Moravian Sugar Cookies
1 lb. dark chocolate chips
1/2 c. pistachios, chopped
1/2 c. roasted salted almonds, chopped
1/2 c. hazelnuts, chopped
1/2 c. dried apricots, chopped
1/2 c. golden raisins
1/2 c. dried cherries, chopped

Linzertorte Cookies

With Moravian Sugar Cookies & Raspberry Preserves

For the Linzertortes
Spread a thin layer of the jam on a cookie. Top with another cookie to make a sandwich. Dust with confectioners sugar.

For the plating
Serve on a platter with other assorted petit fours to accompany tea, coffee or aperitif service.

Ingredients

1 sm tube Moravian Spice Cookies
1 sm jar raspberry preserves
confectioners sugar

Lemon Cheesecake
Made with Moravian Lemon Cookie Crust

For the Crust
Combine all ingredients in a mixing bowl until well mixed. Using a flat-bottomed glass, firmly press the crumb mixture into a 9" Pyrex pie plate. Place in refrigerator to chill.

For the Filling
Beat all ingredients in a mixing bowl with a hand mixer until light and fluffy. Pour the filling into the chilled pie crust. Refrigerate for at least 2 1/2 hours to allow to set.

For the Plating
Slice the cheesecake and place on a plate with a few stewed peaches and fresh raspberries.

The Crumb Crust Technique
This crumb crust works for baked and unbaked pie recipes. The many flavors of the Moravian Cookie Crumbles open a new world of creativity.

Adding Salt to Sweet
Some sweet things need a little salt to make them taste rich, such as pie crust, caramel and cookies.

Ingredients

For the Crust
1 c. Moravian Lemon Cookie Crumbs
1/4 c. unsalted butter, melted
1 tbsp. brown sugar
pinch salt

For the Filling
8 oz. cream cheese, softened
14 oz. condensed milk
zest of 1 lemon, minced
1/2 c. fresh squeezed lemon juice

Lemon Cheesecake

Pumpkin Cheesecake

Made with Moravian Pumpkin Spice Cookies

For the Crust
In a large mixing bowl, combine crumbs and butter. Mix. You should be able to squeeze a handful of crumbs together and maintain shape when fully mixed. Press into the bottom of a well greased spring-form pan, using a flat-bottomed pan or glass to evenly distribute the crust mix and pack it down. Refrigerate.

For the Filling
Beat all ingredients in a mixing bowl with a hand mixer until light and fluffy. Pour the filling into the chilled crust. Refrigerate for at least 2 1/2 hours to allow to set.

For the Plating
Slice the cheesecake and place on a small dessert plate with whipped cream and pecan pralines.

Ingredients

For the Crust
1 c. Moravian Spice Cookie Crumbles
1/4 c. unsalted butter, melted
1 tbsp. brown sugar
pinch salt

For the Filling
8 oz. cream cheese, softened
14 oz. condensed milk
One 15-oz. can pumpkin pie filling
2 tbsp. brown sugar
2 tsp. cinnamon
pinch cloves
pinch allspice

Pumpkin Cheesecake

Pumpkin Pie

Made with Moravian Pumpkin Spice Cookie Crust

For the Crust

Combine all ingredients in a mixing bowl until well mixed. Using a flat bottomed glass, firmly press the crumb mixture into a 9" Pyrex pie pan. Bake at 350° for 7-10 minutes and allow to rest.

For the Filling

Mix the sugar, salt, spices and flour in a large mixing bowl. Stir in the syrup, pumpkin and milk. Let rest overnight to develop flavor. Blend in the eggs before filling the crust pan. Bake at 400° for 40-45 minutes until filling is set but soft. Chill.

For the Plating

Slice the pie and serve on a plate with whipped cream and more of the Moravian Pumpkin Spice Cookies.

Ingredients

For the Crust
2 c. Pumpkin Spice Cookie Crumbles
1/4 c. unsalted butter, melted
1 tsp. brown sugar
pinch salt

For the Filling
2 oz. sugar
2 oz. brown sugar
1 1/2 tsp. salt
1 1/2 tsp. ground cinnamon
3/4 tsp. ground ginger
3/4 tsp. fresh ground nutmeg
1 tbsp. bread flour
3 oz. corn syrup
One 12 oz. can pumpkin pie filling
2 c. milk
1/2 c. eggs

Magic Bars

Made with Moravian Sugar Cookie Crust

For the Crust
Combine all ingredients in a mixing bowl until well mixed. Using a flat bottomed glass, firmly press the crumb mixture into a 12" Pyrex casserole dish. Place in refrigerator to chill.

For the Topping
Pour the condensed milk over the crust. Sprinkle with the other ingredients. Bake at 350° for 15-25 minutes until toasted and molten. Allow to cool completely before cutting bars.

For the Plating
Serve on a platter with other assorted cookies and cakes as a holiday dessert spread.

Ingredients

For the Crust
2 c. Moravian Sugar Cookie Crumbles
1/2 c. unsalted butter, melted
1 tsp. brown sugar
pinch salt

For the Topping
Two 14 oz. cans sweetened condensed milk
1 c. milk chocolate chips
1 c. butterscotch chips
1 c. pecans, chopped
1 c. hazelnuts, chopped
1 c. macadamia nuts, chopped

Crystallized Berry Tart
Made with Moravian Tangerine Orange Cookie Crust

For the Pastry Cream
Split the vanilla bean lengthwise and scrape the seeds into the cream. In the saucepan, over medium heat, add the vanilla bean and sugar to cream and bring to a simmer. In a mixing bowl, whisk together the egg yolks and slowly drizzle into the hot cream, whisking vigorously until half the cream has been added to the eggs. Add the egg mixture back into the remaining cream, reduce the heat to low and continue to whisk vigorously until sauce is noticeably thicker. Remove from heat and transfer to a cool container to stop the mixture from continuing to cook. Place in the refrigerator to chill for at least two hours.

For the Crust
Mix all ingredients in a mixing bowl and then press into a fluted tart pan. Refrigerate.

For the Tart
Fill the tart shell with pastry cream and smooth with a spatula. Arrange berries in a circular fashion around the tart, beginning in the center with the smaller blueberries. Follow with the raspberries, then blackberries and finally strawberries. Put the sugar and honey in a saucepan with enough water to form a runny sludge. Cook over medium high heat to a hard crack stage (when you stick a fork in it and press it up and down on a plate, strings of sugar form and stand). Remove from the heat and wait for sugar to stop boiling. Using a spoon, drizzle sugar glaze over berries and allow to set for 5-6 minutes while glaze hardens.

For the Plating
Cut a slice of the tart and plate it with a dollop of whipped cream and fresh berries marinated in lemon juice and sugar..

Ingredients

For the Pastry Cream
1 vanilla bean
3 c. heavy cream
3/4 c. sugar
6 egg yolks

For the Crust
1 1/4 c. Moravian Tangerine Orange Cookie Crumbles
3 oz. unsalted butter, melted
pinch of salt

For the Tart
1 pt. strawberries
1 pt. blackberries
1 pt. raspberries
1 pt. blueberries
1 c. sugar
2-3 drops honey

Crystallized Berry Tart

Apple Brown Betty
Made with Moravian Spice Cookie Crust & Rum Raisin Ice Cream

For the Topping
Begin by whipping butter with a hand mixer until slightly creamy. Add brown sugar and continue to mix. Add cookie crumbles and pinch of salt. The mixture should form large clumps.

For the Filling
Combine apples and lemon juice in mixing bowl and toss. Add the remaining ingredients and toss to coat. Pour into a deep casserole dish and top with topping mixture. Bake at 350° for 35-45 minutes or until top is browned and filling is bubbling around the edges.

For the Plating
Allow the Brown Betty to rest before serving. This allows the juices to thicken. Spoon into bowls and serve with rum raisin or butter pecan ice cream.

On Brown Betty
Brown Betty became popular in the 1950s as a quick, made from scratch dessert. It is typically classified as a cobbler and characterized by the streusel topping, usually made by adding flour to butter and seasoning. A delicious twist: Moravian Spice Cookies make a much more flavorful topping for this dish.

Ingredients

For the Topping
1 1/2 sticks unsalted butter,
   at room temperature
2 c. Moravian Spice Cookie Crumbles
1/4 c. brown sugar
pinch salt

For the Filling
7-10 Granny Smith apples, cut into
   wedges
juice of 1/2 lemon
1/2 c. dried cherries
1/2 c. dried cranberries
2 tbsp. cinnamon
1/4 c. brown sugar

Black Forest Trifle

Made with Stewed Cherries, Moravian Double Chocolate Cookies, Whipped Cream & Chocolate Pudding

For the Stewed Cherries
Combine all ingredients in a saucepan and bring to a simmer for 15-18 minutes, until juice is reduced to a glaze and clinging to the cherries. Place in refrigerator to chill.

For the Trifle
In a deep, clear casserole dish, cover the bottom with crushed cookies. Follow with layers of chocolate pudding, then stewed cherries and whipped topping. Continue alternating layers with remaining ingredients.

For the Plating
Spoon a portion of the trifle into a bowl and top with a dollop of whipped topping, crushed cookies and stewed cherries.

Ingredients

For the Stewed Cherries
Two 16 oz. bags frozen cherries, thawed
1/2 c. sugar
juice of 1/2 lemon
dash almond extract

For the Trifle
2 lrg boxes chocolate pudding, prepared according to directions
1 med container whipped topping
2 tubes Moravian Double Chocolate Cookies, coarsely broken

Grilled Peaches

Made with Peach Ice Cream & Moravian Lemon Cookies

For the Peaches
Dip cut side of peaches into rum and then into brown sugar. Grill peaches on hot grill for 2-4 minutes. Turn 45° and grill for an additional 2-4 minutes.

For the Plating
Place the grilled peaches in a bowl while still warm. Top with two large scoops of peach ice cream. Garnish with Moravian Lemon Cookies.

Ingredients

4 peaches, halved & pitted
1/4 c. Captain Morgan spiced rum
1/4 c. brown sugar
Moravian Lemon Cookies

Grilled Peaches

Moravian Spice Cookie Haystacks

For the Haystacks

Melt the butterscotch chips in a double boiler or microwave and pour over the noodles, cookie pieces, peanuts and toffee pieces. Toss to coat. Using a spoon, drop mixture onto wax paper into small piles placed on the countertop and let cool. Once solidified, store in an airtight container or bag.

For the Plating

Serve on a platter with an assortment of other sweets. Great served alongside coffee or tea.

Ingredients

12 oz. butterscotch chips
1 1/2 c. crunchy chow mein noodles
1 1/2 c. Moravian Spice Cookies, broken into pieces
1/2 c. toffee pieces
1/4 c. honey roasted peanuts

Haystacks

Moravian Cookie Granola

For the Granola
Toss all ingredients in a large mixing bowl until evenly mixed. Store in a large plastic bag in the cupboard.

For the Plating
Serve for breakfast with milk or yogurt and fresh berries, peaches or bananas.

Ingredients

4 c. honey oat clusters or rolled oats, lightly toasted
2 c. puffed wheat cereal
1 c. Moravian Cranberry Orange Cookies, broken into small pieces
1/4 c. raisins
1/4 c. golden raisins
1/2 c. dried cranberries
1/2 c. dried apples, diced
1/2 c. toasted almond slivers
1/2 c. toasted pecans
1/2 c. honey roasted peanuts

Moravian Key Lime Cookie Crusted Bananas

For the Bananas
Dredge the bananas in the flour, then the egg wash and finally in the cookie crumbles. Deep fry at 350° until golden brown and crispy.

For the Plating
Serve the fried bananas with whipped cream and raspberry preserves.

Ingredients

4 large firm bananas (not too ripe)
1/2 c. flour
3 eggs, beaten with 1/2 c. milk
2 c. Moravian Key Lime Cookie
    Crumbles

Chocolate Marshmallow Cookies

Chocolate Covered Moravian Sugar Cookie & Marshmallow Fluff Sandwiches

For the Cookie Sandwiches

In a double boiler, melt chocolate in a mixing bowl, stirring constantly until completely melted and smooth. Remove from heat and continue to stir for 8-10 minutes until slightly cooler. Make sandwiches by smearing a small amount of the fluff between two cookies. Top with a little more fluff. Dip finished cookies in chocolate slightly more than halfway. Allow to cool. Use tongs to dip cookies into chocolate a second time to completely cover cookies. Place cookies on wax paper and allow to cool completely before packing in tins.

Moonpie™ & RC Cola™

Moonpies™ are a prized confection in the South, especially the Carolinas. Nothing goes better with a Moonpie™ than a Royal Crown Cola™. It's a match made in heaven.

Ingredients

2 tubes Moravian Sugar Cookies
1 jar marshmallow fluff
1 lb. dark chocolate

Marshmallow Cookies

Homemade Cereal Bars

Made with Dried Fruits & Moravian Tangerine, Orange-Cranberry, & Key Lime Cookies

For the Bars

In a large mixing bowl, combine and toss all ingredients except corn syrup and marshmallows. In a saucepan, bring the corn syrup to a simmer and add the marshmallows. Continue to stir until the marshmallows are melted. Pour corn syrup mixture over the cereal, fruit and cookies. Toss to coat. Transfer to a glass 11 x 6 x 2-inch baking dish. Allow to cool for 30 minutes. Cut into bars.

Make Your Own Candy Bars

Smear some peanut butter on one side of these and dip in chocolate to make your own candy bars.

Ingredients

1 c. Cheerios
1 c. Rice Chex
1 c. corn flakes
1/2 c. dried apples
1/2 c. dried cranberries
1/2 c. dried cherries
1/2 c. raisins
1/2 c. Moravian Tangerine Cookies, crushed
1/2 c. Moravian Orange-Cranberry Cookies, crushed
1/2 c. Moravian Key Lime Cookies, crushed
1/2 c. light corn syrup
16 oz. marshmallows

For the Candy Bars
peanut butter
semi-sweet chocolate

Homemade Cereal Bars

Cherries Jubilee
Made with Moravian Spice Cookie Whipped Cream

For the Whipped Cream
In a mixer, beat chilled cream, vanilla extract and sugar on high with whisk attachment until cream has stiff peaks. With a rubber spatula, fold in 1/4 cup of the cookie crumbles and refrigerate.

For the Cherries Jubilee
Combine all ingredients in a medium saucepan and simmer over medium low heat for 15-20 minutes. Keep warm.

For the Plating
Spoon some of the warm cherries into a bowl and top with some of the whipped cream. Finish by sprinkling the remaining 1/4 cup of cookie crumbs.

Ingredients

For the Whipped Cream
2 c. heavy cream
1/4 c. confectioners sugar
1/2 tbsp. real vanilla extract
1/2 c. Moravian Spice Cookie
  Crumbles

For the Cherries Jubilee
2 c. fresh dark cherries, pitted
1 oz. Kirsch or plain brandy
1/3 c. sugar
1/4 tsp. almond extract
1/4 c. orange juice
1/4 tsp. cinnamon

Lemon Bars

Made with Moravian Lemon Cookie Crust

For the Crust

Combine all ingredients in a mixing bowl until well mixed. Using a flat bottomed glass, firmly press the crumb mixture into an 8"x 8" Pyrex casserole pan. Bake at 350° for 7-10 minutes.

For the Filling

Beat the eggs and sugar in a large bowl with a mixer until smooth. Fold in the lemon zest and juice. Stir to incorporate. Fold the flour in last with a spatula. Pour over the crust. Bake at 350° for 20 minutes or until filling is set. Remove and place on a wire rack to cool. Once completely cool, dust with powdered sugar and cut into squares.

For the Plating

Serve in a stack on a large platter with other assorted petit fours. Garnish with candied lemon slices.

Ingredients

For the Crust
2 c. Moravian Lemon Cookie Crumbles
1/4 c. unsalted butter, melted
1 tbsp. brown sugar
pinch salt

For the Filling
1 c. sugar
2 eggs, beaten well
1 tbsp. grated lemon zest
1/3 c. fresh squeezed lemon juice
2 tbsp. all purpose flour

Cookie Sandwiches

Butter Cream Cookie Sandwiches, Key Lime Pie Cookie Sandwiches & Lemon Cream Drop Cookie Sandwiches

For The Butter Cream Filling (makes 3 lbs.)

Place the egg whites in a mixer and beat with cream of tartar until peaks are stiff. While egg whites are beating, cook sugar and water in small saucepan to hard crack stage. Slowly drizzle sugar into egg whites while beating on medium speed until completely mixed and creamy. Place in a bowl and reserve. Place the butter in the mixer and beat on high speed until light and fluffy. Gently fold in the meringue and flavor accordingly.

For the Butter Cream Sandwiches

Flavor one pound of the Butter Cream with 1 teaspoon vanilla extract, 2 teaspoons spiced rum and a pinch of salt. Place in a zip-lock bag and cut off one small corner or tip. Squeeze approximately one teaspoon of Butter Cream on the back of a cookie and top with a second cookie. Press down to evenly spread filling. Repeat. Store in the refrigerator.

For the Key Lime Pie Cookie Sandwiches

Flavor one pound of the Butter Cream with one tablespoon lime extract. Place in a zip-lock bag and cut off one small corner or tip. Squeeze approximately one teaspoon of Butter Cream on the back of a cookie and top with a second cookie. Press down to evenly spread filling. Repeat. Store in the refrigerator.

For the Lemon Cream Drop Cookie Sandwiches

Flavor one pound of the Butter Cream with one teaspoon lemon extract. Place in a zip-lock bag and cut off one small corner or tip. Squeeze approximately one teaspoon of Butter Cream on the back of a cookie and top with a second cookie. Press down to evenly spread filling. Repeat. Store in the refrigerator.

Ingredients

For the Butter Cream Filling
11 oz. sugar
1/4 c. water
8 egg whites
pinch cream of tartar
2 lbs. unsalted butter,
    room temperature
flavorings (below for each sandwich)

For the Butter Cream Sandwich
1 tbsp. vanilla extract
2 tsp. spiced rum
salt
Moravian Sugar Cookies

For the Key Lime Pie Sandwich
1 tbsp. key lime extract
Moravian Key Lime Cookies

For the Lemon Cream Drop Sandwich
1 tbsp. lemon extract
Moravian Lemon Cookies

Cookie Sandwiches

Apple Fritters

For the Fritters

Combine all ingredients in a mixing bowl and mix together. Form rough 2" balls of mixture and dust with more cookie crumbles. Deep fry at 350° until crispy (5-7 minutes). Remove from fryer and drain on a paper towel.

For the Plating

Serve the fritters on a plate dusted with cinnamon and confectioners sugar.

Ingredients

4 Granny Smith apples, peeled & grated
4 oz. cream cheese, softened
2 eggs
1/2 c. heavy cream
2 tsp. cinnamon
1/2 c. Moravian Cranberry Orange Cookie Crumbles

Apple Fritters

Featured WEEKENDS RECIPES

Salem Baking's Weekend recipes are intended for the more deft of hand, perfect for a couple's evening at home or family get together. Entertaining is both enjoyable and easy with Moravian cookies, which bring these incredible dishes to life in new ways. Get the kids involved and create something special, or just enjoy yourself in the kitchen.

Weekends

Pâté de Campagne

With Pistachios, Courvoisier & Moravian Spice Cookies

For the Pâté

Combine all the ingredients except for the bacon and bay leaves in a mixing bowl over an ice bath. Line a loaf pan with overlapping pieces of bacon, cutting strips long enough to fit the ends. Place a small amount of the pâté mixture into the pan, so you can set the first strips of bacon for the ends in place. Repeat process until loaf pan has been filled and bacon is covering three sides. Fold bacon over pâté mix and use scissors to trim the excess. Place bay leaves on top. Place loaf pan in a larger casserole dish filled to 3/4 the height of the loaf pan and bake at 325° for 1 1/2 hours or until internal temperature reaches 150°. Place in the refrigerator to chill for 2 1/2 hours. Remove pâté from pan and scrape off any excess fat. Wrap tightly in plastic wrap.

For the Plating

Serve slices of the pâté with grain mustard, chopped raw shallot, cornichons, chopped hard-boiled egg, capers or caper berries and toast points.

On Pâté

Pâté is the original potted meat, an incredibly delicious cold meatloaf-like creation that is delicately savory with a hint of sweet spice. This recipe is relatively simple and the final result rewarding. Pâté is best enjoyed as a first course with the accompaniments or in a small salad of arugula dressed with olive oil and lemon juice.

Ingredients

1 1/2 lb. ground pork
4 oz. pork liver, diced
2 oz. yellow onion, fine diced
1 clove garlic, minced
1 tbsp. fresh flat-leaf parsley, chopped
1 1/4 oz. Moravian Spice Cookie
   Crumbles, ground finely
1 egg
1/4 c. pistachios
pinch ground coriander
pinch dried thyme
pinch ground cloves
pinch fresh ground nutmeg
1/3 oz. salt
1/4 tsp. white pepper
1 oz. Courvoisier
2 oz. heavy cream
bacon, as needed
8 bay leaves

Pâte de Campagne

Italian Wedding Soup

For the Meatballs
Sweat the onions and garlic in a sauté pan over medium heat for 10-12 minutes. Add the herbs to the onions. Add this mixture to the beef, along with the pine nuts, rice, eggs and cookie crumbles. Season with salt and pepper. Fry a small piece of the mix to check for seasoning. Adjust if necessary. Form meat mix into 1/2 oz. balls and bake on a parchment lined sheet pan at 400° for 10-15 minutes until browned and cooked through.

For the Soup
Bring all ingredients except the herbs to a simmer over medium high heat. Reduce to medium low and let simmer for 30-45 minutes until the vegetables are tender and the flavors marry. Add the herbs and let steep. Season with salt and pepper.

For the Plating
Ladle the soup into a bowl over a few of the meatballs and some cooked orzo pasta.

Ingredients

For the Meatballs
1/2 c. yellow onion, diced small & sweated in olive oil
2 cloves garlic, minced
1 tsp. fresh rosemary, chopped
1 tsp. fresh thyme, chopped
1 tsp. fresh oregano, chopped
1 lb. ground beef
1/4 c. toasted pine nuts
1/2 c. cooked rice
4 eggs, beaten
1/2 c. Moravian Spice Cookie Crumbles, ground finely
salt & pepper

For the Soup
2 qts. chicken broth
1 med yellow onion, diced
2 ribs celery, diced
2 med carrots, peeled & diced
1/2 head large cabbage, chopped
2 large cans stewed tomatoes
2 cans white cannellini beans
1 oz. fresh basil, thinly sliced
1 tbsp. fresh rosemary, chopped
1 tbsp. fresh thyme, chopped
1 tbsp. fresh oregano, chopped
salt & pepper

Italian Wedding Soup

Stuffed Cabbage Rolls
Made with Savory Moravian Spice Cookie Stuffing

For the Tomato Sauce
In a saucepan over medium heat, sweat onions and garlic in olive oil until translucent (7-9 minutes). Add the crushed tomatoes, wine, bay leaves and chicken broth. Stir to incorporate. Reduce heat to medium low and simmer, stirring often to prevent sauce from sticking or scorching (20-25 minutes). Once the sauce is reduced and noticeably thicker, season with salt and pepper to taste. Add the chopped herbs and remove from heat.

For the Filling
Sweat the onions, shallots and garlic in a sautépan with some olive oil until translucent (5-7 minutes). Finish at the last minute with the herbs and caraway. Cook until fragrant (2-3 minutes) and allow to cool. Mix with all remaining ingredients in a bowl and work with your hands to evenly incorporate all ingredients. Place in refrigerator covered and allow to rest for 10-15 minutes.

For the Rolls
Remove the first few outer cabbage leaves if necessary. Core the cabbage by cutting a cone around the core into the cabbage, leaving the head intact. Make sure all of the core is removed. Place the cabbage into a large stockpot with boiling salted water and watch carefully, checking every minute or so to remove the blanched outer leaves. Place in a colander to drain. Once you have removed all of the leaves large enough to stuff, discard the cabbage core. To stuff the leaves, place a small (3 oz.) portion of the filling on the inside of the leaf, slightly above the vein. Roll the vein portion of the leaf over the meat stuffing and fold in the sides of the leaf as tightly as possible. Roll over to rest on the upper third of the leaf. Place in a large casserole dish in a bed of tomato sauce. Repeat until all the stuffing is used. Once all the leaves are stuffed and in the casserole dish, top with more of the tomato sauce and bake at 350° for 30-40 minutes.

For the Plating
Place a pair of the cabbage rolls on a plate with some rice pilaf. Dress with a little more of the sauce on top. Serve with a crusty sourdough bread.

How do I know if my raw beef mixture is properly seasoned?
To test the seasoning of the beef mixture, cook a small spoonful in boiling water and taste to check the seasoning.

Ingredients

For the Tomato Sauce
1/4 c. olive oil
1 lrg yellow onion, diced small
3 cloves garlic, minced
3 lrg cans crushed tomatoes
1/2 c. dry white wine
4 bay leaves
2 cans chicken broth
2 tsp. fresh oregano, chopped
2 tsp. fresh flat-leaf parsley, chopped
salt & pepper

For the Filling
1 lrg yellow onion, diced small
2 cloves garlic, minced
2 shallots, minced
2 tsp. fresh rosemary, chopped
2 tsp. fresh thyme, chopped
2 tsp. fresh flat-leaf parsley, chopped
1/2 tsp. caraway seed cracked in a
   spice grinder
1/2 c. cooked rice
1 lb. ground beef
1 lb. fresh ground pork sausage (mild
   Italian works well)
2 eggs, beaten well
1/2 c. Moravian Spice Cookie
   Crumbles
salt & pepper

For the Rolls
2 lrg heads savoy or green cabbage
   filling

Scalloped Potatoes
Made with Moravian Spice Cookie Crumb Topping

For the Potatoes
Mix the cream with the garlic, shallots and herbs. Slice the peeled potatoes thinly, using a v-shaped slicer. Place some of the sliced potatoes in the bottom of a large shallow casserole dish. Drizzle with the cream. Season with salt and pepper. Sprinkle with a little cheese. Repeat layer by layer until dish is filled, trying to make the top as flat as possible by pressing the potatoes down into the mix.

For the Crumb Topping
Combine all ingredients and spread over the top of the casserole. Cover with foil and bake at 375° 45-60 minutes. Remove foil. Turn oven to broil and continue to bake for 3-5 minutes until golden brown.

For the Plating
Serve a generous spoonful of potatoes alongside roast chicken, turkey or pork.

Ingredients

For the Potatoes
4 lrg russet potatoes, peeled
2 c. heavy cream
2 cloves garlic, minced
1 lrg shallot, minced
1 tsp. fresh rosemary, chopped
1 tsp. fresh thyme, chopped
salt & pepper
1/2 c. shredded Asiago cheese

For the Crumb Topping
1 oz. unsalted butter, melted
1 c. Italian seasoned bread crumbs
1/4 c. Moravian Spice Cookie
  Crumbles
1/4 c. Asiago, shredded
1/4 c. shredded sharp white cheddar
1 tbsp. fresh flat leaf parsley, chopped
salt & pepper

Stuffed Zucchini

Made with Stewed Beef, Rice, Moravian Spice Cookies & Parmigiano

For the Stuffing

Start by searing the beef in a medium stock pot or Dutch oven over medium high heat. Add onions, celery, carrots and garlic. Sauté 2-3 minutes until softened. Add the tomatoes, beef broth, red wine and rosemary. Let simmer 2-3 hours loosely covered on medium low, stirring often to prevent sticking. Once sauce is reduced and quite thick and the meat is falling apart, shred the meat in a mixer with paddle attachment. Season with salt and pepper. Add the cooked rice, cookie crumbles and Parmigiano to the mix. Stir to incorporate all ingredients. Allow to rest 5-7 minutes, allowing cookies to absorb the liquid. Adjust the seasoning if necessary.

For the Zucchini

Begin by preparing a tomato sauce. In a large saucepan, cook the onions, garlic and Italian seasoning in the olive oil on medium heat. Once the onions are transparent, add the tomatoes and wine. Allow to simmer 45-50 minutes. Add the basil and allow to steep off the heat for 10 minutes. Season sauce with salt and pepper. Set aside. With a paring knife, carefully cut the core out of the zucchini leaving a little at the bottom in order to make a small cup to hold the stuffing. Fill the zucchini with the stuffing mix and set aside. In a large casserole dish, layer the bottom of dish with tomato sauce and place the stuffed zucchini on top of sauce. Top the stuffed zucchini with more cookie crumbles and Parmigiano. Bake covered at 375° for 25-30 minutes. Uncover and bake an additional 10-15 minutes until topping is browned and squash is tender.

For the Plating

Serve three zucchini on a plate in a pool of the sauce. Serve alongside rice pilaf.

Ingredients

For the Stuffing

2 lb. beef, cut for stew
1 med yellow onion, diced
1 rib celery, diced
1 sm carrot, diced
2 cloves garlic, minced
1 lrg can tomatoes, diced
One 14 oz. can beef broth
1 c. red wine
2 tsp. fresh rosemary, chopped
salt & pepper
1 c. cooked rice
1/2 c. Moravian Spice Cookie
  Crumbles
1 c. grated Parmigiano

For the Zucchini

3 tbsp. extra virgin olive oil
1 med yellow onion, diced small
4 cloves garlic, minced
1 tbsp. Italian seasoning
2 lrg cans tomatoes, diced
1 c. white wine
2 tbsp. fresh basil, chopped
salt & pepper
pinch sugar
1 tbsp. fresh oregano, chopped
4 12" zucchini, trimmed & cut into
  3" lengths
1/4 c. Moravian Spice Cookie
  Crumbles
1/4 c. grated Parmigiano

Stuffed Zucchini

Moravian Key Lime Cookie Crusted Crab Stuffed Risotto Fritters
Made with Spicy Saffron Sauce

For the Sauce
In a saucepan, reduce the wine with the saffron over medium low heat until almost dry (1 1/2 hours). This process extracts the most flavor from the saffron. (For ideal results, put the saffron in the wine in a glass 2-3 days beforehand to get as much flavor as possible.) Add the saffron reduction to the mayonnaise along with all other ingredients and mix well.

For the Risotto
In a medium stock pot over medium heat, add some olive oil and cook the onions until translucent (3-5 minutes). Add the rice and continue to cook and stir for 2-3 minutes. Add the chicken stock bit by bit, constantly stirring, allowing the last addition of liquid to be absorbed before adding the next. Once you have the first three cups of chicken broth in the pot, begin tasting every so often to check progress. You should feel a slight resistance to the bite, without any crunch. Season finished risotto with salt and pepper. Spread on a sheet pan lined with plastic wrap. Refrigerate to cool. Can be made two days in advance.

For the Stuffing
Mix all ingredients in a mixing bowl and refrigerate. Can be made one day in advance.

For the Fritters
Begin by making a small sheet of the risotto, pressing some of it into your hand (It helps if your hands are slightly wet to keep the risotto from sticking). Place a small ball of the crab mix in the center of the risotto sheet and then form the risotto around the filling by closing your hand. Gently pat the fritter to make sure the stuffing is completely enclosed. Roll in key lime cookie crumbles. Once all fritters have been completed, deep fry at 375° until golden brown (4-5 minutes).

For the Plating
Serve the risotto fritters with a salad of greens dressed with vinaigrette or with sautéed spinach and broccolini. Spread the sauce near the rim of the plate on opposite sides, Place the accompaniment (salad or vegetables) at the center of the plate. Place the fritters around the accompaniment.

Ingredients

For the Sauce
1/2 c. white wine
pinch saffron
1/2 c. mayonnaise
1 clove garlic, minced fine
1 tbsp. Asian chili paste (look for the one with the rooster)
dash white wine vinegar
pinch fresh flat-leaf parsley, chopped

For the Risotto
olive oil
1 medium yellow onion, diced finely
2 c. Arborio rice
4-5 c. chicken broth
salt & pepper

For the Stuffing
1/2 c. mayonnaise
2 tbsp. sour cream
4 scallions, greens & whites, sliced thin
3 tbsp. parmesan cheese
4 lrg basil leaves, chopped
1/4 c. toasted pine nuts
1 lb. backfin crabmeat

For the Fritters
risotto
stuffing
3 c. Moravian Key Lime Cookie Crumbles

Crab Risotto Fritters

Sauerbraten

German Style Pot Roast with Moravian Spice Cookie Sauce

For the Roast

Mix the seasonings. Save half for the braising mix and use half to season beef. Brown in a large sautépan. Deglaze pan with beef broth. Add roast and juices to a deep roasting pan.

For the Vegetables

Add liquids and remaining half of seasonings to pot with roast and bake covered at 300° for two hours. Add vegetables and continue cooking until meat is fork tender. Remove meat from pan and strain juices into a saucepan. Reserve vegetables to serve with the roast.

For the Sauce

Bring the roasting juices to a boil and add the cookie crumbles into the saucepan bit by bit until you reach desired thickness.

For the Plating

Slice or pull the roast. Serve over mashed or boiled potatoes in a large bowl. Arrange vegetables around the potatoes and spoon on sauce.

On Sauerbraten

Sauerbraten is extremely popular and has a long history in Germany. It was originally made from horse meat, until during the 1200s when the Pope declared horse meat forbidden to Catholics for consumption. In this version, Moravian Spice Cookie Crumbles stand in for the traditional ginger-snaps.

Ingredients

For the Roast
4 tbsp. salt
2 tbsp. pepper
4 tsp. dry mustard
2 tsp. ground cloves
2 tsp. fresh ground nutmeg
2 tsp. ground coriander
4 lb. top-round sirloin
One 14 oz. can beef broth

For the Vegetables
2 cans beef broth
1 c. dry white wine
2 tbsp. red wine vinegar
sauerbraten seasonings
1/2 head large red cabbage, chopped
2 lrg carrots, peeled & thick sliced
1 lrg yellow onion, chopped
2 ribs large celery, chopped
2 lrg parsnips, peeled & thick sliced

For the Sauce
roasting juices
Moravian Spice Cookie Crumbles

Roasted Butternut Squash & Moravian Spice Cookie Ravioli
Made with Sage Brown Butter

For the Pasta Dough
Place the flour in a large mixing bowl. Make a well in the middle of the flour and place the beaten eggs in the well. Mix with hands by swirling in the flour little by little. Knead the dough until smooth. Let it rest in the refrigerator for one hour.

For the Filling
Cut the squash in half and roast at 400° for 45-60 minutes until very tender. While the squash cooks, sweat the onions in a sautépan with olive oil until translucent. Season with the rosemary, salt and pepper. Scrape the pulp of the squash into a food processor and puree until creamy. Add the onions, cookie crumbles and goat cheese and season with salt and pepper. Process again to incorporate all the ingredients.

For the Ravioli
Roll the pasta dough out with a pasta machine or by hand until very thin. Dust with flour. Place a sheet of dough on a ravioli press and fill with the squash puree. Brush the exposed edges of pasta dough with water before topping with another sheet of pasta dough. Press to seal. Cut ravioli. Repeat until all filling is used. Dust with flour to prevent sticking. Blanch the ravioli in boiling water 2-3 minutes. In a large sautépan over medium high heat, add the butter and sage leaves. Swirl until butter is well browned (be careful not to burn). Add a dash of sherry vinegar. Finally, add ravioli and toss to coat.

For the Plating
Plate the ravioli in large wide bowls dressed with the sauce, garnish with cooked sage leaves and top with grated Asiago cheese.

Ingredients

For the Pasta Dough
1 lb. semolina or bread (high gluten) flour
6 eggs, beaten well
pinch salt
water, as needed

For the Filling
3 lrg butternut squash
1 sm yellow onion, diced small
 olive oil
2 tsp. fresh rosemary, chopped
salt & pepper
1/2 c. Moravian Spice Cookie Crumbles
3 oz. goat cheese

For the Ravioli
pasta dough
filling
8 oz. unsalted butter
3 sprigs sage
dash sherry or apple cider vinegar

Grilled Pork Tenderloin

Made with Moravian Tangerine Cookie-Nut Streusel topped Sweet Potato Casserole, Balsamic Swiss Chard & Port Wine-Sour Cherry Sauce

For the Streusel Topping
Place all ingredients except butter in a mixing bowl and toss. Drizzle butter over mix and toss to coat and distribute. Season with a pinch of salt.

For the Casserole
To prepare sweet potatoes, bake at 400° for 45 minutes to an hour (or until a knife can pass through the center easily) on an aluminum foil lined cookie sheet. Cut cooked potatoes in half and remove skin (should be fairly well separated from the sweet potato). Place pulp in mixing bowl and mash with fork or beat with mixer on medium until smooth and creamy. Add butter and vanilla extract and mix again to incorporate. Season with salt to taste. Place mash in a baking dish and top with streusel mixture. Bake at 375° for 20 minutes or until topping is browned and bubbly.

For the Port Wine Sauce
Bring wine to a boil and reduce to a simmer. Add cherries and reduce to 1/4 the original volume. Allow to cool slightly.

For the Pork Tenderloins
Season pork with salt and pepper. Grill for 10-12 minutes or until cooked through. Allow to rest.

For the Balsamic Swiss Chard
Heat a large sautépan over medium high heat. Add olive oil, shallots and chard. Saute 4-6 minutes until chard is wilted. Season with salt and pepper to taste. Drizzle in balsamic vinegar and toss.

For the Plating
Spoon out a serving of the casserole with the topping intact. Make a small bed of wilted chard in front of the casserole. Top with 1/2 of the sliced pork tenderloin. Lightly drizzle the reduced wine sauce over the pork and around the plate.

On Chard
Swiss chard & rainbow chard are not only beautiful, but also very healthful and tasty. The trick to cooking chard and making it taste good is to cook it just until it wilts. Chard contains iron compounds, and when exposed to moisture and air can oxidize and make taste overly earthy or bitter. When properly prepared, chard is much more flavorful, healthful and beautiful than spinach.

Ingredients

For the Streusel Topping
1/2 c. hazelnuts, finely chopped
1/2 c. pecans, finely chopped
1/2 c. Moravian Tangerine Cookie Crumbles
1/4 c. granola
1/4 c. brown sugar
2 tsp. cinnamon
1 stick (4 oz.) unsalted butter, melted

For the Casserole
6 lrg sweet potatoes, baked whole
1/4 lb. unsalted butter
1 tbsp. vanilla extract
salt

For the Port Wine Sauce
1 bottle port wine
1/2 c. dried sour cherries

For the Pork Tenderloin
2 pork tenderloins
salt & pepper

For the Balsamic Swiss Chard
1 lrg bunch Swiss chard or rainbow chard, destemmed, 1/2" sliced & rinsed
1 tbsp. olive oil
1 large shallot, diced fine
2 tsp. balsamic vinegar
salt & pepper

Grilled Pork Tenderloin

Key Lime Grouper

Moravian Key Lime Cookie Crusted Grouper with Gemstone Potatoes Confit, Roasted Asparagus & Lemon Caper Butter Sauce

For the Gemstone Potatoes Confit

Place potatoes, shallots, garlic, bay leaves and seasonings in medium saucepan or a small, deep, ovenproof casserole dish. Pour in just enough olive oil to cover everything completely. Place loosely covered dish in oven at 300° for 1 1/2 hours or until potatoes are tender. Drain well with a slotted spoon and place on a plate lined with paper towels to absorb excess oil. Heat a large nonstick skillet over medium high heat. Once hot, drizzle a little of the cooking oil in the pan and place potatoes cut side down. Sear until crispy on one side (about 4-6 minutes). Flip and toss with salt, pepper and fresh chopped herbs. Reserve warm.

For the Asparagus

Trim ends of asparagus and place on foil-lined cookie sheet. Drizzle lightly with olive oil. Season with salt and pepper. Place in oven at 400° for 8-12 minutes until tips are slightly crispy and stalks are tender. Reserve warm.

For the Fish

Season filets with salt and pepper. Make slurry by mixing the flour and water together. Lightly coat the flesh side of the filets with slurry and dredge the slurry side in the cookie crumbles. Place on a lightly sprayed cookie sheet lined with foil and bake at 400° for 12-16 minutes until fish is cooked through and flaky. (If crust starts to get too dark, cover loosely with foil to finish cooking.)

For the Sauce

In a small saucepan, bring juice, zest, wine, shallots and garlic to a rapid simmer. Reduce until almost dry. Remove from heat and whisk in butter one tablespoon at a time until it reaches a creamy sauce consistency. Strain into sauce boat. Finish with capers and fresh herbs. Salt and pepper to taste.

For the Plating

Place a small flat bed of the asparagus on the plate. Top with fish at a slight angle. Loosely scatter potatoes around the plate. Spoon the caper sauce over the fish and loosely drizzle sauce around the plate.

Ingredients

For the Gemstone Potatoes Confit
3 lb. gemstone/fingerling potatoes or baby potatoes, halved lengthwise
2 med shallots
6 cloves garlic
4 bay leaves
lots of fresh herbs: rosemary, thyme, sage, parsley (chop & reserve some of the herbs, & leave the remainder in whole sprigs)
2 to 3 c. olive oil (extra virgin would be too strong)

For the Asparagus
1 bunch asparagus
extra virgin olive oil

For the Fish
Four 6 oz. portions of grouper (or other meaty white fish)
2 c. Moravian Key Lime Cookie Crumbles
1/4 c. flour
1/4 c. water

For the Sauce
2 lemons, zested & juiced
1/2 c. dry white wine
1 med shallot, chopped
2 sm cloves garlic, halved
1 stick unsalted butter
2 tbsp. capers
fresh chopped herbs

Key Lime Grouper

Chicken Paprikash

Made with Moravian Spice Cookie Sauce & White Beans with Bacon & Onions

For the Beans
In a wide saucepan, fry bacon pieces over medium heat until crispy. Strain with a slotted spoon and reserve. In the bacon grease, sauté the vegetables until translucent. Add the beans and herbs. Simmer for 15-20 minutes over low heat. Season with salt and pepper to taste.

For the Chicken and Sauce
Place the chicken in a plastic bag with the first set of seasonings and a bit of olive oil. Seal and toss to coat all pieces evenly. In a large sauté pan over medium high heat, brown the chicken breast skin side down for 5-7 minutes. Flip to brown the other side. Transfer to a foil-lined sheet pan and finish in oven at 400° for 8-10 minutes. In the pan the chicken was seared, add everything for the sauce except the chicken broth and sauté for 5-7 minutes over medium heat until onions are translucent. Add the chicken broth. Reduce to 2/3 original volume. Add the cookie crumbles to the sauce to thicken. Simmer 3-4 minutes on low heat. Remove the bay leaves and cinnamon sticks.

For the Plating
Place a large spoonful of the white beans in a wide bowl. Top with small, diced raw onion and crispy bacon. Place a finished chicken breast on top of the beans. Top with sauce.

Ingredients

For the Beans
4 oz. thick sliced smoked slab bacon, cut into small pieces
1/2 med yellow onion, diced small
1/2 rib celery, diced small
1/2 sm carrot, peeled & diced small
1 clove garlic, minced
2 cans white beans (navy or cannelini)
pinch fresh rosemary, thyme & sage, chopped
salt & pepper

For the Chicken
Four 8 oz. chicken supremes (also known as airline breasts, boneless breast with the first joint of the wing still connected)
2 tbsp. Hungarian paprika
1 tbsp. salt
1/2 tbsp. black pepper
2 tsp. fresh thyme, chopped

For the Sauce
2 med yellow onions
2 cloves garlic, minced
1 tbsp. paprika
2 tsp. fresh thyme, chopped
4 bay leaves
3 cinnamon sticks
pinch ground clove
2 c. chicken broth
1/4 c. Moravian Spice Cookie Crumbles, ground fine
salt & pepper

Crispy Moravian Lemon Cookie Crusted Catfish

Made with Spicy Remoulade

For the Sauce
Mix all ingredients in a large mixing bowl until evenly incorporated and refrigerate.

For the Catfish
Season the filets with salt and pepper. Dredge in flour, dip in egg-milk mixture, and finish by breading with cookie crumbles. Pan fry in butter over medium high heat until golden brown (5-7 minutes). Flip and finish frying. Season the fried fish with Cajun seasoning.

For the Plating
Serve the catfish with slaw and corn on the cob with a spoonful of the remoulade sauce on the fish.

Ingredients

For the Sauce
1/2 c. mayonnaise
2 tbsp. Dijon mustard
1 tsp. shallot, minced
1 tsp. fresh tarragon, chopped
juice of 1/2 lemon
1 1/2 tbsp. Sriracha hot sauce

For the Catfish
Four 7 oz. catfish filets
1 c. flour
2 eggs
1/2 c. milk
2 c. seasoned bread crumbs
1/2 c. Moravian Lemon Cookie
   Crumbles
Cajun seasoning

Moussaka

For the Filling
Begin by browning the beef in a large skillet over medium high heat. Once water has cooked off (10-15 minutes), add the onion to fry with the beef until translucent. Add the garlic, followed by the tomatoes and seasonings. Continue to simmer. Allow the juice from the tomatoes to evaporate and the tomato paste to mix in well (20-30 minutes). Add the cookie crumbles to thicken the meat ragout. Set aside.

For the Béchamel Sauce
In a saucepan over medium heat, melt butter. Add flour and cook for 3-4 minutes. Begin adding milk one cup at a time, whisking in the first cup before adding the next. Once all milk has been added, season with salt, pepper, and nutmeg. Finish with the cheese.

For the Moussaka
In a large, deep casserole dish sprayed with pan coating, layer potatoes on the bottom of the pan. Follow with the zucchini, then tomatoes and spinach. Sprinkle with the feta, pine nuts and golden raisins. Top with eggplant. Top with the meat ragout and finally the sauce. Bake at 350° for 60-90 minutes. Let rest 20 minutes before cutting to allow to set up.

For the Plating
Cut squares and scoop onto a plate. Serve with marinara sauce and garlic bread.

On Moussaka
Moussaka could be considered the national dish of Greece. The casserole of meat ragout, eggplant and béchamel sauce is a tribute to the ingenuity of peasants taking the meager ingredients they had on hand and elevating them to an ethereal level. The origins of the dish, however, are widely debated. The Greeks claim it as their own, and the Turks dispute this claim. However, most food historians agree that the eggplant made its way to the Mediterranean by way of Moorish invaders and the classic seasoning is common throughout the Maghrib (North African Mediterranean Coast) and the Middle East.

Ingredients

For the Filling
2 lb. ground beef
1 med yellow onion, diced
2 cloves garlic, minced
1 lrg can diced tomatoes
1 tbsp. paprika
4 bay leaves (remove after cooking)
2 tsp. fresh rosemary, chopped
2 tsp. fresh thyme, chopped
2 tsp. fresh oregano, chopped
2 tsp. cumin
2 tsp. cinnamon
3 tsp. tomato paste
1/2 c. Moravian Spice Cookie Crumbles
salt & pepper

For the Béchamel Sauce
1/2 c. unsalted butter
1/2 c. flour
4 c. whole milk
1/2 c. Pecorino Romano cheese
fresh nutmeg, grated

For the Moussaka
4 Russet potatoes, peeled & sliced thin
2 zucchini, sliced thin
3 eggplant, sliced thin, laid out, salted & patted dry
4 tomatoes, sliced
12 oz. spinach, sautéed & drained
2 med yellow onions, sliced, sautéed in olive oil, seasoned with a pinch of dill
1/2 c. feta cheese
1/4 c. toasted pine nuts
1/4 c. golden raisins

Moussaka

Moravian Tangerine Cookie Crusted Tilapia Gujonettes

Made with Peanut Dressed Jicama-Dandelion Slaw

For the Gujonnettes
Season the tilapia filets with salt and pepper. Dredge in the flour, dip in the egg wash, and finally dip into the cookie crumbles to coat. Fry in a deep fryer at 350° for 8- 10 minutes until crunchy, golden and cooked through.

For the Peanut Dressing
Combine all ingredients in a mixing bowl and whisk together. Thin with water if necessary.

For the Jicama Dandelion Slaw
Toss the slaw mix with some of the dressing and set aside.

For the Plating
Pile some of the slaw on the plate. Lean some of the gujonettes onto the slaw. Serve some of the peanut sauce on the side.

Ingredients

For the Gujonnettes
4 tilapia filets, cut into strips
1/2 c. flour
2 eggs, beaten with a 1/2 c. milk
3 c. Moravian Tangerine Cookie Crumbles
salt & pepper

For the Peanut Dressing
1/2 c. peanut butter, crunchy
1/4 c. soy sauce
1/2 c. sweet chili sauce
water (to thin)

For the Jicama Dandelion Slaw
1 lrg jicama, cut into thin strips
1 red bell pepper, sliced thin
4 scallions, sliced thin
1 bunch dandelion greens
1/4 bunch fresh cilantro, rough chopped

Braised Pork Porterhouse

Made with Root Beer Glaze, Melted Onions & Moravian Spice Cookie Bread Pudding

For the Chops
Season the porterhouses liberally with salt and pepper. In a large braising pan over medium high heat, sear the porterhouses 8-10 minutes. Add the sliced onions and cook until translucent. Add the root beer and broth. Place in oven at 350° for one hour until liquid has reduced to a glaze and onions are extremely wilted. Finish sauce with a dash of cider vinegar and teaspoon of butter.

For the Stuffing
Sauté shallots and celery in butter. Pour over bread cubes. Add the raisins and cookies and toss to coat. Season with salt and pepper. Mix cream, herbs and eggs. Pour over bread mixture, toss to coat and allow the bread to soak up the liquid. Season with salt and pepper. Pour mix into square casserole dish and bake at 350° for one hour until top is browned and custard is set. Allow to rest 10-15 minutes.

For the Plating
Place the porterhouse chop on a large platter. Add a scoop of the stuffing, so that it touches the side of the chop. Pile onions on top of the chop and spoon on finished glaze. Drizzle glaze around the plate presentation.

Ingredients

For the Chops
Four 16 oz. pork porterhouse chops
4 sweet yellow onions, thinly sliced
One 16 oz. can root beer
One 14 oz. can chicken broth
dash cider vinegar
1 tbsp. unsalted butter

For the Stuffing
3 lrg shallots, diced
1 rib celery, diced
1/4 c. raisins, soaked in 3 oz. Bourbon
4 c. stale French bread, cut into cubes
1/2 c. Moravian Spice Cookies, broken into small pieces
1 tsp. fresh rosemary, chopped
1 tsp. fresh sage, chopped
1 tsp. fresh thyme, chopped
2 c. heavy cream
3 eggs, beaten

Moravian Vanilla Walnut Crusted Torte

Made with D'Anjou Pears, Goat Cheese, Rosemary, & Honey

For the Crust

In a large mixing bowl, combine cookie crumbles and butter. Mix well. Using a flat-bottomed container, firmly press the crumbs into a lightly greased fluted tart pan. Set aside.

For the Torte

Cut pears in half lengthwise and core them with a melon baller. Place pears cut side down and slice 1/3" thick sections. Place sliced pear half in the tart pan with the tip pointing toward the center and gently press with your palm to create an even fan with the pears. Repeat with the other three pear halves, each going in the pan directly across from the others. Top sliced, fanned pears with crumbled goat cheese, drizzle with honey and sprinkle with chopped rosemary. Bake at 350° for 20-25 minutes until cheese is slightly brown on top.

For the Plating

Cut torte into eight slices. Serve each slice with a dollop of sour cream sweetened with confectioners' sugar and seasoned with a touch of vanilla extract.

Goat Cheese, Honey & Rosemary?

This combination of flavors is very complementary. Try making a spread with the three for use on bread (especially scones) instead of butter or as a dip for fresh fruit.

Ingredients

For the Crust
1 c. Moravian Vanilla Walnut Cookie Crumbles
3/4 stick unsalted butter, melted

For the Torte
2 D'Anjou pears, sliced
1 tbsp. fresh rosemary, chopped
2 tbsp. honey
2 oz. goat cheese, crumbled

Vanilla Walnut Torte

Moravian Spice Cookie Crumb Cake
With Buttermilk Cream Cheese Icing

For the Crumb Topping
Mix all ingredients in a mixing bowl.

For the Sweet Dough
Mix the water and yeast with a pinch of sugar. Dissolve the yeast and allow to rest. Add the eggs and malt. Mix. In a mixer fitted with a dough hook, mix the yeast mixture with other ingredients on low until dough forms. Switch to high speed for 6-8 minutes until dough is elastic and smooth. Place in refrigerator and allow to rest for 30 minutes. Break the dough in half and stretch to fit in two 12" buttered casserole dishes. Brush the surface of the bread with a mixture of one egg yolk and two tablespoons milk, beaten together. Allow dough to proof at room temperature for 2 hours. Bake at 375° for 20-25 minutes until golden brown. Remove from oven and top with the crumb topping. Return to the oven for an additional 10 minutes to brown the top. Allow to rest 10-15 minutes.

For the Icing
Mix with a mixer until creamy. Refrigerate.

For the Plating
Place the frosting in a sandwich bag. Clip one of the corners with scissors, so you can pipe out the icing. Cut the cake into squares and top with a drizzle of the icing.

Ingredients

For the Crumb Topping
1/4 c. unsalted butter,
  at room temperature
3 tbsp. brown sugar
pinch salt
2 tbsp. flour
1/4 c. Moravian Spice Cookie
  Crumbles
1/4 c. oats
2 tbsp. almond slices, toasted
2 tsp. ground cinnamon
fresh grated nutmeg

For the Sweet Dough
2 c. very warm (but not hot) water
1 1/2 oz. dry yeast
4 eggs beaten
1 oz. malted milk powder
4 oz. cake flour
1 lb. plus 3 tbsp. bread flour
2 pinches salt
2 oz. sugar
pinch cinnamon
fresh grated nutmeg
4 oz. unsalted butter

For the Icing
8 oz. cream cheese, softened
1/2 c. buttermilk
3 tsp. brown sugar
1 tsp. vanilla extract

Cookie Crumb Cake

White Chocolate Mousse & Moravian Lemon Cookie Trifle
Made with Fresh Berries

For the White Chocolate Mousse
Place sugar in a small saucepan and add just enough water to make a runny sludge. Add a drop of honey to prevent the sugar from crystallizing during cooking. Bring to a boil over medium high heat and cook to hard-crack stage (when you stick a fork in it and press it up and down on a plate, strings of sugar form and stand). While sugar is cooking, whip egg whites with pinch of tartar (keeps meringues from falling) to create stiff peaks (when the cream is very thick and semisolid). Drizzle in cooked sugar while whipping on high. Place mixture in refrigerator to chill.

Place chocolate in a medium mixing bowl and place over a saucepan of boiling water (saucepan should be wide enough for half of the mixing bowl to fit in the water). Occasionally stir with a rubber spatula until chocolate is completely melted and smooth. Allow the chocolate to rest 3-4 minutes while stirring occasionally. Using a rubber spatula, gently fold the chocolate into the egg white mixture and return to the refrigerator to chill slightly.

Put cream in mixer and beat on high to create stiff peaks. Then place in the refrigerator to chill slightly. Fold the two mixtures together with a rubber spatula and place in the refrigerator to set for at least two hours. This mousse can be made four days in advance and stored in the refrigerator.

For the Trifle
Place rinsed berries, lemon juice and sugar in a large mixing bowl. Toss to coat. Let rest in refrigerator for 10-15 minutes while flavor develops. In a trifle dish (or another large clear glass dish), begin by creating a thin layer with some of the cookies (just enough to cover the bottom with some cookies overlapping). Put mousse in a large freezer bag and cut off a small tip and one of the bottom corners to create a makeshift pastry bag, Squeeze mousse into dish in a circular fashion, working from the outside in until all cookies have been covered. Spoon on just enough berry mixture to cover the mousse. Repeat the layers with remaining ingredients. Garnish with fresh berries, whipped cream and fresh mint.

About the Mousse
This mousse is a great base recipe, as the flavorings can be changed according to your own creativity, However, if you decide to use milk or dark chocolate for the mousse, use only 3/4 the normal amount because of the difference in stability.

Ingredients

For the Mousse
5 egg whites
pinch cream of tartar
1/2 c. sugar
water
2 c. heavy cream
1 lb. white chocolate (dark chocolate may be substituted using 3/4 of 1 lb.)

For the Trifle
2 c. fresh berries; raspberries, black berries, strawberries and blueberries
1 lemon juice
2 tbsp. sugar
2 sleeves Moravian Lemon Cookies

Moravian Spice Cookie Ice Cream
Made with Caramel Apple Swirl

For the Caramel Apple Swirl
Bring the sugar, water and honey to a boil. Once boiling, do not mix. Cook the sugar mixture until it turns a deep amber color and then slowly add the cream. (Be very careful, as the sugar is extremely hot.) Once the cream has been added, add the apples and cinnamon and stir to incorporate. Allow the mixture to chill in the refrigerator while you make the ice cream base.

For the Ice Cream Base
Split the vanilla beans lengthwise and scrape the seeds with a knife. Add the seeds and bean pods to the cream, milk and sugar in a saucepan. Bring to a simmer over medium heat. Whisk the egg yolks in a mixing bowl until frothy. Add a little of the cream mixture to the eggs, whisking to incorporate. Gradually add more and more of the cream to the yolks, whisking to incorporate each addition. Once you have added 1/4 of the cream mixture to the yolks, add the yolk mix back to the cream in the saucepan. Continue to whisk until mixture coats the back of a spoon. Strain the base to remove the seed pods and reserve.

For the Ice Cream
Place the ice cream base in the ice cream machine and spin according to machine directions. Once the ice cream mixture is almost ready, add the broken cookies, allowing the machine to incorporate the cookie pieces. Add the caramel swirl and spin a bit longer to swirl the ice cream with the caramel.

For the Plating
Place three scoops in an attractive glass bowl and garnish with additional caramel sauce warmed and a few of the cookies.

Ingredients

For the Caramel Apple Swirl
1 c. sugar
1/2 c. water
3-4 drops of honey
3/4 c. heavy cream
1 Golden Delicious apple, diced
2 tsp. cinnamon

For the Ice Cream Base
3 vanilla beans
1 qt. heavy cream
1 qt. whole milk
1 1/4 lb. sugar
20 egg yolks

For the Ice Cream
ice cream base
caramel apple swirl
1/2 large tube of Moravian Spice Cookies, broken into pieces

Balsamic Berry Cobbler
Made with Granola-Spice Cookie Streusel & Bailey's Whipped Cream

For the Cobbler
Combine all ingredients in a large bowl and reserve.

For the Streusel Topping
Combine in a bowl and reserve.

For the Whipped Cream
Bring Bailey's to boil in a medium sautépan and lower to a slow simmer. Reduce to 1/4 of original volume, approximately 12-15 minutes. Place reduced Bailey's in refrigerator to cool. Begin beating chilled heavy cream in a large bowl with a hand mixer and whisk attachments on medium high. Once cream starts to thicken and aerate (approximately 8-10 minutes, but be careful not to over mix). Reduce speed to medium and start drizzling in chilled Bailey's reduction. Mix in remaining Bailey's and place in refrigerator to chill.

Preheat oven to 350°. Pour cobbler mix into deep 6 x 6 inch casserole dish. Top with streusel mix. Bake for 20-25 minutes until bubbly around the edges and toasted on top. Allow to set and cool for 15-20 minutes (This allows the juice to thicken). Scoop into bowls and top with whipped cream before serving.

Ingredients

For the Cobbler
2 pt. fresh raspberries
2 pt. fresh blueberries
2 pt. fresh blackberries
1 lemon, zest grated and juiced
1 c. sugar
1/4 c. balsamic vinegar

For the Streusel Topping
1 c. granola
1 c. crushed Moravian Spice Cookies

For the Whipped Cream
1 c. Bailey's Irish Cream
2 c. heavy cream
1/4 c. confectioners sugar

Berry Cobbler

Moravian Spice Cookie Crusted French Toast Bananas Foster
Made with Butter Rum Caramel

For the Butter Rum Caramel
Begin by melting butter in a saucepan over medium heat. Cook in the sugar until it becomes runny and bubbly and slightly changes color. Add the rum, schnapps and vanilla extract and allow to simmer 12-15 minutes. (Use extreme caution when adding alcohol to a hot sauce, which makes the alcohol extremely flammable.) Finish by adding a pinch of salt.

For the Stuffed French Toast
Mix the cinnamon and sugar together. Set aside. Make sandwiches by spreading cream cheese on two pieces of bread. Sprinkle liberally with cinnamon and sugar. Sandwich two pieces of banana in between them. Make a batter by beating two eggs with a cup of milk. Dip sandwiches in batter and dredge in the cookie crumbles. Fry the sandwiches in butter in a sauté pan on medium heat until golden brown. Flip and finish cooking the other side.

For the Plating
Cut the sandwich in half at an angle. Prop one half of the sandwich on top of the other. Top with warm rum sauce, sliced bananas and whipped cream.

On Bananas Foster
Bananas Foster is a famous dessert that originated in New Orleans at the restaurant Brennan's. It was named after a wealthy banker. The dish usually includes bananas prepared in a rum sauce with a sweet cake.

Ingredients

For the Butter Rum Caramel
2 oz. unsalted butter
1/2 c. brown sugar
4 oz. Captain Morgan spiced rum
2 oz. banana schnapps
1 tsp. vanilla extract
pinch salt

For the Stuffed French Toast
1 tbsp. cinnamon
2 tbsp. sugar
8 oz. cream cheese, softened
8 slices white bread
2 bananas, halved & sliced lengthwise
2 eggs, beaten
1 c. milk
1 1/2 c. Moravian Spice Cookie Crumbles

Stuffed French Toast

Coffee Cream Cheese Squares
Made with Moravian Double Chocolate Cookie Crust

For the Crust
Combine all ingredients in a mixing bowl until well mixed. Using a flat bottomed glass, firmly press the crumb mixture into a 12" Pyrex casserole dish. Place in refrigerator to chill.

For the Filling
Beat all ingredients in a mixing bowl with a hand mixer until light and fluffy. Pour the filling into the chilled pie crust. Refrigerate for at least 2 1/2 hours to allow to set up.

For the Plating
Cut into 2 1/2" squares. Top each with a chocolate covered espresso bean.

Ingredients

For the Crust
2 c. Moravian Double Chocolate Cookie Crumbles
1/4 c. espresso beans, rough chopped
1/4 c. unsalted butter, melted
1 tbsp. brown sugar
pinch salt

For the Filling
16 oz. cream cheese, softened
28 oz. condensed milk
3 tbsp. coffee extract
2 tbsp. Kahlua liqueur

Banana Nut Bread

Made with Moravian Spice Cookies

For the Bread

Combine all ingredients except eggs in a mixer on medium low until dough is evenly mixed. One by one, add the eggs until all are incorporated. Pour the dough into a loaf pan and bake at 350° for 45-60 minutes, until a toothpick inserted in the middle comes out clean.

For the Plating

Serve the bread sliced with honey butter for breakfast.

Ingredients

8 oz. cake flour
3 oz. Moravian Spice Cookie Crumbles
3 1/4 oz. shortening
pinch of grated orange zest
6 1/2 oz. brown sugar
1 tsp. salt
1 1/2 tsp. baking powder
7 oz. ripe bananas, mashed
3 1/2 tbsp. honey
1/2 c. eggs
1 1/2 oz. pecans, chopped
1 tsp. vanilla extract

Vanilla Walnut Truffles
Made with Moravian Vanilla Walnut Cookies

For the Truffle Filling
After bringing cream to a boil, pour it over the chocolate in a mixing bowl. Wrap it with plastic wrap and let rest for 10-15 minutes while chocolate melts. Once chocolate is completely melted, unwrap and begin folding the heavy cream into the chocolate by stirring and folding with a spatula. Wait 10-15 minutes and allow the mixture to cool slightly. Once the chocolate mixture is almost room temperature and is noticeably thicker, fold in the liqueur and cookie crumbles. Refrigerate to harden for at least 2 1/2 hours. Scoop the hardened chocolate mixture using a small 1/2 oz. scoop (referred to as a 40 scoop at your local restaurant supply store) and roll between your hands to form truffle balls. Place onto a wax paper-lined sheet pan and place in freezer to set for 45 minutes.

For the Coating
Melt the chocolate in a double boiler over medium heat, stirring constantly with a spatula. Once the chocolate is completely melted and smooth, remove from heat and continue stirring with spatula, allowing chocolate to cool slightly. Pick up slightly frozen truffle balls by inserting a toothpick. Dip them in the melted chocolate and place on a sheet pan lined with wax paper. Top each with a walnut half and allow to dry/harden for 45 minutes. Once hardened, place in tins and refrigerate for storage. Prior to serving, allow truffles to return to room temperature.

For the Plating
Serve on a platter alongside goat cheese whipped with honey and rosemary.

Ingredients

For the Truffle Filling
2 c. heavy cream
1 lb. fine semi-sweet chocolate
2 1/2 oz. Nocella liqueur
1 c. Moravian Vanilla Walnut Cookie Crumbles

For the Coating
1 lb. fine semi-sweet chocolate
2-3 c. walnut halves

For the Plating
goat cheese
honey
rosemary

Vanilla Walnut Truffles

White Chocolate & Lemon Truffle
Made with Moravian Lemon Cookie Crumbles

For the Truffle Filling
After bringing cream to a boil, pour it over the chocolate in a mixing bowl. Wrap it with plastic wrap and let rest 10-15 minutes while chocolate melts. Unwrap chocolate when it is completely melted, begin incorporating the heavy cream into the chocolate by stirring and folding with a spatula. Allow 10-15 minutes to cool slightly. Once the chocolate mixture is almost room temperature and noticeably thicker, fold in the liqueur and the cookie crumbles. Refrigerate to harden at least 2 1/2 hours. Scoop the hardened chocolate mixture using a small 1/2 oz. scoop (referred to as a 40 scoop at your local restaurant supply store) and roll between your hands to form truffle balls. Place onto a wax paper-lined sheet pan and place in freezer to set for 45 minutes.

For the Coating
Melt the chocolate in a double boiler over medium heat, stirring constantly with a spatula. Once completely melted and smooth, remove from heat and continue stirring with spatula, allowing chocolate to cool slightly. Pick up slightly frozen truffle balls by inserting a toothpick. Dip them into the melted chocolate and place on a sheet pan lined with wax paper. Allow to dry and harden for 45 minutes. Once hardened, place in tins and refrigerate for storage. Prior to serving, allow truffles to return to room temperature.

Ingredients

For the Truffle Filling
1 lb. fine white chocolate
1 1/2 c. heavy cream
2 1/2 oz. limoncello liqueur
1 tsp. lemon extract
1 c. Moravian Lemon Cookie Crumbles

For the Coating
1 lb. fine white chocolate

Lemon Truffles

Rice Pudding
Made with Moravian Cranberry Orange Cookies

For the Rice Pudding
Bring rice, milk, seasonings, salt and sugar to a simmer in a large saucepan over medium heat. Cook constantly, stirring until rice absorbs most of the milk and the mix becomes thick and creamy. Add the cranberries and vanilla. Remove from heat. Beat the egg yolks in a bowl and add a little bit of the hot pudding to the yolks. Stir to incorporate. Pour the yolks into the pudding and fold in quickly. Continue to stir vigorously 10-15 minutes to allow steam to escape. This will help the texture of the finished pudding.

For the Trifle
Serve the pudding warm with a sprinkle of cinnamon and powdered sugar, or serve cold with whipped cream. Garnish with plenty of Moravian Cranberry Orange Cookies.

Ingredients

6 oz. rice
6 3/4 c. milk
1/4 tsp. fresh grated nutmeg
1/4 tsp. ground cinnamon
grated zest of 1/2 orange
1/4 tsp. salt
6 oz. sugar
8 oz. dried cranberries
1 tsp. vanilla extract
3 egg yolks
Moravian Cranberry Orange Cookies

Sticky Buns
Made with Moravian Cookie Crumble Topping

For the Topping
Begin by whipping butter with a hand mixer until lightly creamy. Add brown sugar and continue to mix. Add cookie crumbles and pinch of salt while mixing (should form large clumps).

For the Sweet Dough
Mix the water and yeast with a pinch of sugar. Dissolve the yeast and allow to rest. Add the eggs and malt. Mix. In a mixer fitted with a dough hook, mix the yeast mixture with the other ingredients on low speed until dough forms. Switch to high for 6-8 minutes until dough is elastic and smooth. Place in refrigerator and allow to rest for 30 minutes. Roll the dough out to a square, and cut into strips. Brush the strips with melted butter and sprinkle with the topping. Brush the surface of the dough with a mixture of 1 egg yolk and 2 tablespoons of milk, beaten together. Allow dough to proof at room temperature for 2 hours. Bake at 375° for 20-25 minutes until golden brown. Remove from the oven and top with the crumb topping. Return to the oven for an additional 10 minutes to brown the top. Allow to rest 10-15 minutes.

Ingredients

For the Topping
1 1/2 sticks unsalted butter,
room temperature
2 c. Moravian Spice Cookie Crumbles
1/2 cup brown sugar
pinch salt

For the Sweet Dough
2 c. very warm (but not hot) water
1.5 oz. dry yeast
4 oz. eggs, beaten well
1 oz. malted milk powder
4 oz. cake flour
1 lb. plus 3 tbsp. bread flour
2 pinches salt
2 oz. sugar
pinch cinnamon
fresh grated nutmeg
4 oz. unsalted butter

Cranberry Orange Truffles

Made with Port glazed Cranberries & Moravian Cranberry Orange Cookies

For the Truffle Filling

Place cranberries, zest and port wine in a saucepan. Bring to a simmer and cook until almost completely dry. Set aside and cool. After bringing cream to a boil, pour it over the chocolate in a mixing bowl. Wrap it with plastic wrap and let rest 10- 15 minutes allowing chocolate to melt. Unwrap. Once chocolate is completely melted, begin incorporating the heavy cream into the chocolate by stirring and folding with a spatula for 10- 15 minutes. Allow to cool slightly. Once the chocolate mix is almost room temperature and noticeably thicker, fold in the cranberries and cookie crumbles. Refrigerate to harden at least 2 1/2 hours. Scoop the hardened chocolate mixture using a small 1/2 oz. scoop (referred to as a 40 scoop at your local restaurant supply store) and roll between your hands to form truffle balls. Place onto a wax paper-lined sheet pan and place in freezer to set for 45 minutes.

For the Coating

Melt the chocolate in a double boiler over medium heat, stirring constantly with a spatula. Once completely melted and smooth, remove from heat and continue stirring with spatula, allowing chocolate to cool slightly. Pick up slightly frozen truffle balls by inserting a toothpick. Dip in the melted chocolate and place them on a sheet pan lined with wax paper. Allow to dry and harden 45 minutes. Once hardened, place in tins and refrigerate for storage. Prior to serving, allow truffles to return to room temperature.

Ingredients

For the Truffle Filling
1 lb. fine semi-sweet chocolate
2 c. heavy cream
1/2 c. dried cranberries
1 c. port wine
grated zest of 1 orange
1 c. Moravian Cranberry Orange
   Cookie Crumbles

For the Coating
1 lb. fine semi-sweet chocolate

Cranberry Orange Truffles

Key Lime Truffles
Made with Moravian Key Lime Cookie Crumbles

For the Truffle Filling
After bringing cream to a boil, pour it over the chocolate in a mixing bowl. Wrap it with plastic wrap and let rest for 10- 15 minutes to allow chocolate to melt. Unwrap. Once chocolate is completely melted, begin incorporating the heavy cream into the chocolate by stirring and folding with a spatula for 10 to 15 minutes. Allow to cool slightly. Once the chocolate mix is almost room temperature and noticeably thicker, fold in the liqueur and cookie crumbles. Refrigerate to harden at least 2 1/2 hours. Scoop the hardened chocolate mixture, using a small 1/2 oz. scoop (referred to as a 40 scoop at your local restaurant supply store) and roll between your hands to form truffle balls. Place onto a wax paper-lined sheet pan and place in freezer to set for 45 minutes.

For the Coating
Melt the chocolate in a double boiler over medium heat, stirring constantly with a spatula. Once completely melted and smooth, remove from heat and continue stirring with spatula, allowing chocolate to cool slightly. Pick up slightly frozen truffle balls by inserting a toothpick. Dip in the melted chocolate and place them on a sheet pan lined with wax paper. Allow to dry and harden 45 minutes. Once hardened, place in tins and refrigerate for storage. Prior to serving, allow truffles to return to room temperature.

For the Plating
Serve on a platter with Moravian Key Lime Cookies topped with cream cheese for a Key lime pie effect.

Ingredients

For the Truffle Filling
2 c. heavy cream
1 lb. fine semi-sweet chocolate
2 1/2 oz. Quarentay Tres liqueur
1 oz. key lime juice
1 c. Moravian Key Lime Cookies and Crumbles

For the Coating
1 lb. fine white chocolate

Key Lime Truffles

Stuffed Poached Pears
Made with Cream Cheese, Balsamic Figs & Moravian Spice Cookies

For the Pears
Bring all the liquids to a simmer over medium heat with the seasonings. Simmer 10-15 minutes to infuse the flavor of the spices into the wine and to cook out some of the alcohol. Place the pears in the liquid and simmer over low heat for 20-25 minutes until they are tender and well colored. Remove the pears from the syrup and return the syrup to rapid simmer over medium high heat. Reduce to 1/2 original volume, strain and set aside. Allow pears to cool. Using a paring knife, cut out a cone-shaped segment from the bottom of the pears, removing the core and seeds and creating a space for the filling. Chill syrup and pears separately in the refrigerator for one hour.

For the Stuffing
Simmer the figs in a medium saucepan with the balsamic vinegar over medium heat until almost dry. Figs should be plump and tender. In a mixing bowl, whip the cream cheese together with the condensed milk with a hand mixer until light and fluffy. Fold in the cookie crumbles and then the stewed figs with a spatula to create a swirl effect. Place in a sandwich bag and cut the tip off bag to pipe in to the cavity of the pears. Allow stuffed pears to chill in refrigerator for 1 1/2 hours to set.

For the Plating
Serve the pears on a plate over a thin pool of the reduced poaching liquid covering the plate. Even the bottom of the pear with a knife and stand it up on the center of the plate. Cut a wedge in the pear and lay it down to show off the filling.

Ingredients

For the Pears
4 Bartlett pears, peeled with stem left on
1 c. water
1 c. sugar
2 c. port wine
1 c. light red wine, such as Zinfandel
2 sticks cinnamon
4 cloves
2 allspice berries
grated zest & juice of 1 orange

For the Stuffing
1/4 c. dried black mission figs, diced
1/4 c. balsamic vinegar
6 oz. cream cheese, softened
1/4 c. sweetened condensed milk
1/4 c. Moravian Spice Cookie Crumbles

Tangerine Chocolate Truffles

Made with Moravian Tangerine Orange Cookies

For the Truffle Filling

After bringing cream to a boil, pour it over the chocolate in a mixing bowl. Wrap it with plastic wrap and let rest 10-15 minutes to allow chocolate to melt. Unwrap. Once chocolate is completely melted, begin incorporating the heavy cream into the chocolate by stirring and folding with a spatula. Allow 10-15 minutes to cool slightly. Once the chocolate mix is almost room temperature and noticeably thicker, fold in the liqueur and the cookie crumbles. Refrigerate to harden at least 2 1/2 hours. Scoop the hardened chocolate mixture using a small 1/2 oz. scoop (referred to as a 40 scoop at your local restaurant supply store) and roll between your hands to form truffle balls. Place onto a wax paper-lined sheet pan and place in freezer to set for 45 minutes.

For the Coating

Melt the chocolate in a double boiler over medium heat stirring constantly with a spatula. Once completely melted and smooth, remove from heat and continue stirring with spatula, allowing chocolate to cool slightly. Pick up slightly frozen truffle balls by inserting a toothpick. Dip them into the melted chocolate and place on a sheet pan lined with wax paper. Allow to dry and harden for 45 minutes. Once hardened, place in tins and refrigerate for storage. Prior to serving, allow truffles to return to room temperature.

For the Plating

Serve with candied orange zest or jellied orange slices.

Ingredients

For the Truffle Filling
1 lb. fine semi-sweet chocolate
2 c. heavy cream
2 1/2 oz. Grand Marnier liqueur
1 c. Moravian Tangerine Orange Cookie
    Crumbles

For the Coating
1 lb. fine semi-sweet chocolate

For the Plating
candied orange zest or jellied
    orange slices

Chocolate Pistachio Crunch Truffles
Made with Moravian Double Chocolate Cookie Crumbles

For the Pistachio Crunch
Line a sheet pan with parchment paper and set aside. Put sugar in a small saucepan with just enough water to form a runny sludge. Add 2-3 drops of honey and bring to a boil. Watch carefully, but do not stir, as sugar boils on medium high. Within 8-10 minutes, the sugar should start changing color as it caramelizes. Once the sugar has reached a golden amber, add pistachios and toss with a spatula. Place on the lined sheet pan and spread with spatula. Sprinkle lightly with kosher salt. Allow to cool and harden for 1 1/2 hours. Break brittle into small chunks and grind in the food processor to a coarse, pebble consistency. Sift to catch all of the larger pieces. Discard or regrind any pieces that are too big. Set aside. Can be made one week in advance.

For the Truffle Filling
After bringing cream to a boil, pour it over the chocolate in a mixing bowl. Wrap with plastic wrap and let rest for 10-15 minutes, allowing chocolate to melt. Unwrap once chocolate is completely melted, begin incorporating the heavy cream into the chocolate by stirring and folding with a spatula (10-15 minutes). Allow to cool slightly. Once the chocolate mix is almost room temperature and noticeably thicker, fold in the liqueur, pistachio crunch and cookie crumbles. Refrigerate to harden at least 2 1/2 hours. Refrigerate to harden at least 2 1/2 hours. Scoop the hardened chocolate mixture using a small 1/2 oz. scoop (referred to as a 40 scoop at your local restaurant supply store) and roll between your hands to form truffle balls. Place onto a wax paper-lined sheet pan and place in freezer to set for 45 minutes.

For the Coating
Melt the chocolate in a double boiler over medium heat, stirring constantly with a spatula. Once completely melted and smooth, remove from heat and continue stirring with spatula, allowing chocolate to cool slightly. Pick up slightly frozen truffle balls by inserting a toothpick. Dip in the melted chocolate and place them on a sheet pan lined with wax paper. Allow to dry and harden 45 minutes. Once hardened, place in tins and refrigerate for storage. Prior to serving, allow truffles to return to room temperature.

For the Plating
Place truffles on a platter with fresh strawberries, Moravian Double Chocolate Cookies and a small dish of whipped cream, garnished with mint.

Ingredients

For the Pistachio Crunch
1 c. pistachios, roasted, salted, shelled
1 1/2 c. sugar
honey
salt

For the Truffle Filling
1 lb. fine dark chocolate
2 c. heavy cream
2 1/2 oz. Tuaca liqueur (optional, but recommended)
2 c. pistachio crunch
1 1/2 c. Moravian Double Chocolate Cookies and Crumbles

For the Coating
1 lb. fine dark chocolate

Chocolate Pistachio Truffles

Featured SPECIAL OCCASION RECIPES

Special times are often marked with special tastes that leave a lasting memory. These Salem Baking Special Occasion recipes are perfect for a holiday dinner, an evening with friends and family, celebrations of anniversaries, and other times that deserve a meal that expresses the significance of the event. Enjoy making these time honored classics, presented in a contemporary fashion with Moravian cookies. A memory well worth the effort required to create it.

Special Occasion

Seared Scallops on Endive Leaf

Made with Exotic Herb Beurre Blanc & Macadamia-Moravian Key Lime Cookie Crumbles

For the Crumble
Combine ingredients in a mixing bowl. Set aside.

For the Beurre Blanc
Reduce wine with shallots, garlic and lemon wedges until almost dry then whisk in butter bit by bit until completely incorporated and creamy. Strain sauce and season with salt and herbs.

For the Scallops
Pat dry and allow to rest on paper towels for at least 10 minutes.

Heat a nonstick sautépan on medium high, drizzle with oil and work in batches so as not to overcrowd. Sear scallops seasoned with salt and pepper until well browned (3-4 minutes). Turn and finish (3-4 minutes).

For the Plating
Cut scallops in half and place on endive leaf. Apply a light spooning of the beurre blanc on the scallop and finish with a sprinkle of the crumbles topping. Serve as hors d'oeuvres.

Rethink the Dish
Instead of making the butter sauce, mix grated lemon and lime and orange zest with some chopped basil, mint, flat-leaf parsley, cilantro and butter. Season with salt and top the scallops with the butter. You can also try the butter and crumb topping with any other white fish grilled, pan seared or baked.

Ingredients

For the Crumble
1/2 c. macadamia nuts, chopped
1 c. Moravian Key Lime Cookie Crumbles

For the Beurre Blanc
1 c. dry white wine
1 large shallot, chopped
2 cloves garlic, halved
1 lemon, 1/4 juiced wedges added to pot
1/2 lb. unsalted butter
salt
1 med sprig thyme
fresh chopped exotic herbs: pineapple sage, lemon balm, mint, cilantro & basil

For the Scallops
8 lrg scallops

Seared Scallops

Escargots in the Classic Style

Made with Garlic-Parsley Butter, Pernod & Moravian Spice Cookie Crumbles

For the Garlic Butter

In a saucepan, simmer the garlic in the cream for 10-12 minutes. Strain, saving the cream to cook the snails. Puree the garlic. Mix garlic with the butter and parsley. Season with salt and pepper. Set aside.

For the Snails

Sauté the snails in a large sauté pan over medium high heat with the butter and shallots. Deglaze the pan with the Pernod. Add a dash of hot sauce and the cream. Continue to simmer the liquid for 3-4 minutes. Place snails in cream in the refrigerator to cool for 15-20 minutes. Once cool, remove snails from the cream and place in their shells. Top with the garlic-parsley butter, just filling the top of the snail shell. Finish by adding a pad of Moravian Spice Cookie Crumbles on top of the butter. Bake at 400° on a bed of kosher salt mixed with fresh sage, rosemary and thyme for 6-8 minutes or until cookie crumbles are browned and butter is bubbling.

For the Plating

Serve four snails per person on a bed of the salt and herbs.

On Escargot

Snails have been a popular food in France since ancient times. The most commonly consumed type of snail is the escargot de Bourgogne or Burgundy snail. Snails are so popular in France, they have special events to eat them. Much like an American oyster roast or barbecue, the Cargolade is a large festive occasion where the main course is tiny European mollusks grilled on a special grill and served with garlic butter and bread.

Ingredients

For the Garlic Butter
4 cloves garlic
1 c. heavy cream
1/2 lb. unsalted butter, softened
2 tbsp. fresh flat-leaf parsley, very finely chopped
salt & pepper

For the Snails
16 lrg Burgundy snails, with shells
2 tbsp. unsalted butter
1 shallot, minced
1 1/2 oz. Pernod liqueur
dash hot sauce
cream, from cooking the garlic
garlic parsley butter
1/4 c. Moravian Spice Cookie Crumbles
kosher salt
fresh sage, rosemary, thyme. chopped
salt & pepper

Escargots

Curry Sweet Potato Soup

Made with Jerked Chicken & Moravian Spice Cookies

For the Soup

To prepare sweet potatoes, bake at 400° for 45 minutes to an hour (or until a knife can pass through the center easily) on an aluminum foil-lined cookie sheet. Cut cooked potatoes in half and remove skin (should be fairly well separated from the sweet potato). Place pulp in mixing bowl and fork mash or beat with a mixer on medium until smooth and creamy. Add butter, cream and curry. Mix again to incorporate. Season with salt to taste.

For the Roasted Vegetables

Coat the chicken breasts with the jerk seasoning and grill until cooked through 10-15 minutes.

For the Plating

Ladle some of the soup into the bowl. Top with half of a grilled chicken breast sliced crosswise and Moravian Spice Cookie Crumbles.

Ingredients

For the Soup
6 lrg sweet potatoes, baked whole
2 - 3 tbsp. curry powder
One 14 oz. can chicken broth
1 qt. heavy cream
1/4 c. unsalted butter
salt to taste

For the Roasted Vegetables
Two 8 oz. chicken breasts, boneless
  and skinless
1/4 tbsp. jerk seasoning
Moravian Spice Cookie Crumbles

Wiener Schnitzel

Viennese Pork Cutlet with Moravian Spice Cookie Crust & Sweet & Sour Braised Cabbage

For the Braised Cabbage

Saute the cabbage and onions in a pan over medium high heat with olive oil until wilted. Add the cranberries, vinegar and sugar. Reduce until almost dry. Season with salt and pepper to taste.

For the Cutlets

First, season the cutlets with salt and pepper. Dredge in flour, dip in egg-milk mixture and finish by breading with cookie crumbs. Pan fry in butter over medium high heat until golden brown (5-7 minutes). Flip and finish frying.

For the Plating

Serve the cutlets alongside the braised cabbage with a spoonful of grain mustard for dipping.

Ingredients

For the Braised Cabbage
1 med head green cabbage, sliced
1 med yellow onion, diced
1/2 c. dried cranberries
1/2 c. cider vinegar
1 tbsp. sugar

For the Cutlets
8 sm pork cutlets
1 c. flour
2 eggs
1/2 c. milk
2 c. seasoned bread crumbs
1/2 c. Moravian Spice Cookie
   Crumbles

Baked Halibut

Made with Cashew-Moravian Tangerine Cookie Crumb Topping & Orange Basil Butter

For the Crust
Combine all ingredients in a mixing bowl and toss. Set aside.

For the Orange Basil Butter
Combine all ingredients in a mixing bowl and mix thoroughly.

For the Halibut
Season with salt and pepper. Sear in a sauté pan with a dash of vegetable oil, flip, then finish in a 375° oven for 12-14 minutes until fish is cooked through completely (but is not dry).

For the Plating
Top fish filets with softened butter and sprinkle liberally with cookie crumb mixture. Serve with steamed asparagus and mashed potatoes.

Ingredients

For the Crust
1 c. Moravian Tangerine Cookie
  Crumbles
1/2 c. cashews, chopped
2 tbsp. unsalted butter, melted
1 tbsp. fresh flat-leaf parsley, chopped
salt & pepper

For the Orange Basil Butter
4 oz. unsalted butter, softened
grated zest & juice of 2 oranges,
  reduced to 1 tbsp.
2 tbsp. basil, chopped
salt & pepper

For the Halibut
Four 6 oz. halibut steaks

Baked Halibut

Roulade of Chicken

Made with Sausage-Apple-Moravian Spice Cookie Stuffing with Pan Gravy

For the Stuffing

Begin by browning the sausage in a sauté pan, breaking it up with a spoon as it cooks. Add the apples, celery and onion. Sauté until onions are translucent and apples are soft. Deglaze with chicken stock. Cook spinach separately with butter, salt and pepper. Strain spinach well and add to the pan with the other vegetables. Mix bread crumbs and cookie crumbles with the herbs and goat cheese to make the stuffing mix. Allow to rest in the refrigerator for 10-15 minutes.

For the Chicken and Gravy

Place chicken supremes in a large freezer bag one at a time and beat with a mallet to flatten. Remove from bag and lay skin side down. Spread stuffing mix on the back of the chicken breast. Roll each chicken breast starting with the bottom tip of the breast and rolling toward the top of the breast. Using butcher's twine, tie off the roll in sections 1" apart. This should create a chicken roll with the two wing tips on either end. Once both are stuffed, rolled and tied, sear chicken rolls in a sauté pan on medium high heat with vegetable oil. Finish in the oven at 375° for 15-18 minutes. Check the meat near the joint for cooking progress (as it's the last to cook through). Once cooked, allow to rest for 10 minutes. While chicken is resting, make a gravy by adding a bit of finely minced onion and celery to the oil in the pan. Cook until translucent and add flour, stirring to incorporate. Add chicken broth slowly and bring to a boil. Season with salt, pepper, rosemary and sage. Garnish with chopped hard-boiled eggs. Remove the strings and slice the chicken into rounds.

For the Plating

Plate sliced chicken by shingling the slices on each other in a pool of the gravy. Serve with brie mashed potatoes and sautéed sugar snap peas.

Ingredients

For the Stuffing
1 lb. sweet Italian sausage, skin removed
1 Golden Delicious apple, diced
1/2 rib celery, diced fine
1/2 med yellow onion, diced fine
1/2 c. chicken broth
6 oz. fresh spinach, cooked & drained
1 tbsp. unsalted butter
salt & pepper
1/2 c. panko bread crumbs
1/2 c. Moravian Spice Cookie Crumbles
1 tsp. fresh rosemary, chopped
1 tsp. fresh sage, chopped
2 oz. goat cheese

For the Chicken and Gravy
2 double-breasted chicken supremes, skin on
1 rib celery, diced fine
1/4 med onion, diced fine
2 - 3 tbsp. flour
1 tsp. fresh sage, chopped
1 tsp. fresh rosemary, chopped

Roulade of Chicken

Beef Tenderloin En Croute

Made with Sausage, Shiitakes & Moravian Spice Cookies

For the Stuffing

Brown the sausage in a large sauté pan over medium high heat for 8-10 minutes. Add the onions, shallots and mushrooms to the pan. Sauté until lightly golden and season with the herbs, salt and pepper. Add the cookie crumbs to create a thick paste.

For the En Croute

Season the tenderloin liberally with salt and pepper. Sear in a skillet over medium high heat for 5-8 minutes on each side, then remove tenderloin and place in refrigerator to cool. Lay three pie crusts out, slightly overlapping each one on a floured counter and roll out the overlapping parts to form one solid rectangle. Spread the stuffing paste onto the top 3/4 of the dough, reserving the bottom 1/4 of the dough for the overlay. Place the beef tenderloin on the pastry and wrap the pastry around the beef. Brush it with the egg wash to seal. Fold and tuck the ends under the bottom. Place on a sheet pan and bake at 400° for 15-18 minutes until pastry is browned.

Ingredients

For the Stuffing

1 lb. spicy Italian sausage, casing removed
1/2 sm yellow onion, diced fine
1 sm shallot, minced
1 c. shiitake mushrooms, sliced
1 tsp. fresh rosemary, chopped
1 tsp. fresh thyme, chopped
salt & pepper
1/2 c. Moravian Spice Cookie Crumbles

For the En Croute

1 beef tenderloin, cleaned, trimmed & tied (ask the butcher)
2 to 3 frozen pie crusts, thawed
stuffing (above)
2 egg yolks, beaten with 1/4 c. milk

Bacon Wrapped Venison Loin

Made with Parsnip Puree, Arugula Salad & Blackberry-Brandy Sauce

For the Steaks & Sauce

Begin by rendering the bacon a little more than halfway in a skillet over medium high heat. Wrap bacon around venison and secure with a toothpick. Season the steaks liberally with salt and pepper. Sear steaks in bacon grease over medium high heat for 5-7 minutes on each side, and then reduce heat to medium, rolling the steaks on their sides to finish the bacon. Once bacon is crisp and steaks are medium rare (finish in the oven for well done), remove from the pan. Add the blackberries and deglaze with the brandy and reduced beef broth. Add salt and pepper. Simmer 7 to 8 minutes to cook out the alcohol. Thicken the sauce with cookie crumbles finely ground.

For the Parsnip Puree

Place the parsnips in a saucepan with approximately 20% of the cream and cover. Bring to a rapid simmer and cook for 15-25 minutes until parsnips are very tender. Place parsnips in a food processor with remaining cream, butter, salt and pepper. Puree for 10-15 minutes until smooth.

For the Plating

Plate a single steak in a pool of the sauce. Spoon some of the sauce onto the steaks. Place a pile of the parsnip puree on the back of the plate and drag the spoon through it in a half circle. Make a small salad of arugula, dressed with olive oil, lemon juice, shaved Parmigiano, salt and pepper. Place salad right beside the steak.

Ingredients

For the Steaks & Sauce
4 thick slices smoked bacon
Four 6 oz. venison loin steaks
salt & pepper
1 c. fresh blackberries
1/4 c. brandy
Two 14 oz. cans beef broth, reduced to 1/4 original volume
2 tbsp. Moravian Spice Cookie Crumbles, finely ground

For the Parsnip Puree
6 large parsnips, peeled & chopped
2 to 3 c. heavy cream
2 tbsp. unsalted butter
salt & pepper

For the Plating
3 oz. arugula
.25 oz. olive oil
1 tsp. lemon juice
shaved Parmigiano cheese
salt & pepper

Stuffed Leg of Lamb

Made with Spinach, Sun-Dried Tomatoes, Dried Figs & Moravian Spice Cookies with Garlic & Lemon Roasted Potatoes

For the Potatoes

Place the potatoes in a casserole dish and toss with all the other ingredients. Cover baking dish with aluminum foil and bake in 350° oven for 30 – 45 minutes or until potatoes are softened. Remove the foil with caution and return to the oven for an additional 20-25 minutes at 425° until potatoes are crispy and chicken broth is completely evaporated.

For the Stuffed Leg of Lamb

Sauté spinach with olive oil, salt and pepper. Strain the juice from the cooked spinach. Mix spinach with sun-dried tomatoes, chopped dried figs, cheese and cookie crumbles. Remove lamb from the mesh bag and unroll. Mix mustard, shallots, garlic and herbs into a paste and smear the paste on the leg of lamb. Season liberally with salt and pepper. Place spinach mixture on lamb and roll up. Tie with butcher's twine. Roast leg of lamb at 350° for 100 minutes or until internal temperature reads 130° for medium. Allow lamb to rest 15 minutes before slicing. Return the roasting pan to the range over medium heat and add beef stock. Stir vigorously with a fork to release particles stuck to pan. Strain the jus and season liberally with salt, pepper and fresh mint if desired.

For the Plating

Place a small portion of the roasted potatoes on the plate. Serve the sliced lamb shingled in front of the potatoes and drizzle with the jus.

Ingredients

For the Potatoes

4 russet potatoes, peeled, cut in half widthwise & then into 1/4 sections
8 cloves garlic
juice of 1 lemon
1 tbsp. fresh rosemary, chopped
1 tsp. fresh oregano, chopped
1 tsp. fresh thyme, chopped
2 tbsp. olive oil
One 14 oz. can chicken broth
salt & pepper

For the Stuffed Leg of Lamb

12 oz. spinach
olive oil
salt & pepper
1/2 c. sun-dried tomatoes, soaked in hot water & cut into strips
1/2 c. dried figs, chopped
1/8 c. Pecorino Romano cheese
1 1/2 c. Moravian Spice Cookie Crumbles
One 4 - 5 lb. boneless leg of lamb
4 tbsp. grain mustard
5 shallots, minced
3 cloves garlic, minced
2 tsp. fresh rosemary, chopped
2 tsp. fresh thyme, chopped
2 tsp. fresh mint, chopped
One 14 oz. can beef broth
fresh mint

Stuffed Leg of Lamb

Braised Lamb Shank

Made with Cinnamon-Onion Sauce, Moravian Spice Cookie Gremolata & Orzo Risotto a la Greca

For the Lamb Shanks

Season lamb shanks with salt and pepper. Sear in a large sauté pan over medium high heat with olive oil. Remove shanks and add onions to the pan. Cook until translucent. Add garlic, bay leaves, spices and broth. Place shanks in a deep baking dish or Crock-Pot with onions, seasonings and broth. Bake loosely covered at 300° for 4-4 1/2 hours or until meat is fork tender (or cook in the Crock-Pot for 8-10 hours on low). Season with salt and pepper. Reserve warm. Can be made three days in advance and kept in the cooking sauce.

For the Risotto

Place a deep pot over medium heat with olive oil and lightly toast the pasta. Add the onion and cook until translucent. While stirring vigorously, add the chicken broth a little at a time allowing the pasta to absorb the liquid before adding more. Taste pasta frequently to check progress while adding liquid. When pasta is cooked to a creamy consistency, finish with tomatoes, scallions, feta and herbs. Season with salt and pepper. Reserve warm.

For the Gremolata

Mix all ingredients together thoroughly. Reserve.

For the Plating

In a large wide bowl, place a serving of the risotto in the center. Top with one of the lamb shanks. Spoon some of the cooking liquid over the lamb. Top with a liberal sprinkling of gremolata on the lamb and around the bowl.

What about Leftovers?

If you happen to have shanks and sauce left over, they make an incredible sandwich. Debone the meat and add it to the sauce. Bring back to a simmer. Toast some pita bread and wrap around meat with shredded lettuce, tomato, feta cheese and garlic-dill sour cream.

Prep Like a Pro

This dish requires a long cooking time for the shanks, so you can start the shanks the night before in the Crock-Pot. Let them cook overnight and put the crock in the refrigerator in the morning. It's actually best if it sits for a while before serving. Reheat it on the range in a medium stockpot while you make the risotto and gremolata.

Ingredients

For the Lamb Shanks
4 med lamb fore shanks
1/4 c. extra virgin olive oil
salt & pepper
4 med yellow onions, diced small
2 cloves garlic
4 bay leaves
4 sticks cinnamon
3 tbsp. paprika
2 tbsp. ground cinnamon
2 tsp. ground cumin
2 tsp. dried thyme
One 14 oz. can beef broth

For the Risotto
1 tbsp. olive oil
8 oz. orzo pasta
1 sm yellow onion
2-3 cans chicken broth
5 Roma tomatoes, diced
1 bunch scallions, sliced thin
1/4 c. feta cheese crumbles
1/2 tbsp. fresh oregano, chopped
1/2 tbsp. fresh basil, chopped
salt & pepper

For the Gremolata
1/2 c. toasted almonds, chopped
1 sm clove garlic, minced
grated zest of 1 orange & 1 lemon
1/4 bunch flat-leaf parsley, chopped finely
2 sprigs fresh mint, chopped finely
1/4 c. Moravian Spice Cookie Crumbles

Braised Lamb Shank

Braised Short Ribs
Made with Roasted Vegetables & Braising Sauce

For the Short Ribs
Season the short ribs heavily with salt and pepper. Brown in a large deep braising pan over medium high heat with olive oil. Once browned, deglaze with wine and broth. Add onions, vegetables, tomatoes and herbs. Bake short ribs at 300° for 3 1/2 hours covered. Remove the lid and remove vegetables, bay leaves and beef with a slotted spoon. Add the cookie crumbles to the liquids and transfer liquid to blender. Puree until smooth.

For the Roasted Vegetables
While short ribs are resting, toss all vegetables except zucchini and yellow squash in a mixing bowl with olive oil, salt and pepper. Place on a sheet pan lined with aluminum foil. Roast in oven at 450° for 15 minutes. Add the zucchini and yellow squash. Continue to roast another 15-20 minutes until vegetables are tender.

For the Plating
Place three short ribs on the plate and drizzle the sauce around the plate. Arrange the roasted vegetables around the meat on the plate.

For a Heartier Meal
Serve the short ribs over polenta for a heartier meal. This also will help turn a dinner for four into a dinner for six guests. The creamy consistency of the sauce makes it a great place to dip bread.

Ingredients

For the Short Ribs
8 meaty beef short ribs
salt & pepper
olive oil
1 c. red wine
Two 14 oz. cans beef broth
12 yellow pearl onions
2 ribs celery, large chopped
2 carrots, peeled & sliced thickly
1 can tomatoes, diced
2 tbsp. fresh rosemary, chopped
2 tsp. fresh thyme, chopped
5 bay leaves
1/2 c. Moravian Spice Cookie Crumbles

For the Roasted Vegetables
4 parsnips, peeled & sliced thickly
4 acorn squash, cut into wedges
2 lrg turnips, peeled & large diced
2 lrg beets, cut into wedges
2 med zucchini, sliced thick on a bias
2 med yellow squash, sliced thickly on a bias
olive oil
salt & pepper

Osso Buco

Made with Fennel, Oranges, Green Olives, Israeli Couscous & Moravian Spice Cookie Sauce

For the Osso Buco

Place the onions, vegetables, tomatoes and orange zest and juice in a large, deep roasting pan. Season with salt and pepper. Drizzle with olive oil and toss to coat. Roast in oven at 400° for 25-30 minutes, stirring often until roasted golden. While the vegetables roast, season the shanks with salt and pepper. Sear shanks in a large sauté pan over medium high heat with dash of olive oil. Once seared, place the shanks in the roasting pan with the roasted vegetables, wine, broth and herbs. Cover lightly with aluminum foil and return to oven at 300° for 2-2 1/2 hours until shanks are fork tender.

Uncover and carefully remove the shanks with a slotted spoon or spatula to a plate. Remove the vegetables (remove the bay leaves and discard). Place vegetables in food processor and process into a smooth paste. Pour the roasting juices in the processor slowly until all is incorporated. Place vegetable and roasting sauce mixture in a saucepan over medium heat. Add the cookies and let simmer 8-10 minutes until thickened (if too thick, thin with beef broth). Add the olives, vinegar and basil. Season to taste with salt & pepper.

For the Plating

Sauté the fennel in a large sauté pan with olive oil over medium high heat until lightly golden. Add the oranges and sauté another 2-3 minutes until oranges have softened. Place some of the Israeli couscous in a wide bowl with some of the sautéed fennel and oranges. Place one of the shanks on the vegetables and cover shank with sauce. Top with a liberal sprinkling of the gremolata.

Ingredients

For the Osso Buco

1 lrg yellow onion, diced
1 rib celery, diced
1 lrg carrot, peeled & diced
1 lrg bulb fennel, stalks trimmed & bulb diced
Two 16 oz. cans diced tomatoes
2 oranges, zested & juiced
salt & pepper
olive oil
Four 10 to 12 oz. veal shank steaks
1 c. red wine
6 c. beef broth
1 tbsp. fresh thyme, chopped
1 tsp. fresh rosemary, chopped
4 bay leaves
1/4 c. Moravian Spice Cookie Crumbles, finely ground
1 c. small green olives, pitted
dash red wine vinegar
1 tbsp. fresh basil, thinly sliced

For the Plating

2 bulbs fennel, stalks trimmed & 1/4" sliced
olive oil
1 orange, cut into 8 wedges
2 c. cooked Israeli couscous, seasoned with olive oil, parsley, salt & pepper
1/4 c. Moravian Spice Cookie Gremolata (page 161)

Kofta

Made with Tabouleh, Flat Breads & Radish-Cucumber Yogurt Sauce

For the Tabouleh
Combine all ingredients in a mixing bowl and toss together. Refrigerate for 15 minutes to allow flavors to marry.

For the Radish-Cucumber Yogurt Sauce
Mix all ingredients in a mixing bowl. Allow to rest in the refrigerator 10-15 minutes to allow the flavors to marry.

For the Kofta
Combine all ingredients by hand, mashing everything together in a mixing bowl. Allow mix to rest in the refrigerator for 10-20 minutes. Form the ground meat mixture into small 4" sausages around skewers and grill (a George Foreman grill works well).

For the Plating
Make a medium mound of tabouleh toward the back of the plate. Place a few toasted flat breads alongside a small salad of shredded iceberg lettuce, sliced tomato, red onion, feta cheese and red wine vinaigrette with grilled koftas.

On Kofta
Kofta are a handmade fresh meat sausage popular in the Middle East and are related to the more familiar gyro of Greek origin.

On Tabouleh
Tabouleh is a grain salad popular in the Middle East and is typically made with some form of cooked grain (usually bulgur wheat), fresh vegetables, dried fruits, nuts and fresh herbs. All ingredients are dressed with olive oil and lemon juice. The combination of dried fruits and nuts in a savory dish is indicative of the Arab style.

Ingredients

For the Tabouleh
1 c. cooked couscous or quinoa
1 c. cooked barley or bulgur wheat
1/2 c. cherry tomatoes, halved
1/2 c. cucumber, peeled & seeded, small diced
5 scallions, greens & whites sliced thin
1 med fennel bulb, diced small
1/4 c. dried figs, diced
1/4 c. golden raisins
1/4 c. dried apricots, diced
1/4 c. toasted pine nuts
1/4 c. toasted almonds, chopped
3 tbsp. fresh flat-leaf parsley, chopped
3 tbsp. fresh mint, chopped
1 1/2 tbsp. fresh cilantro, chopped
1/8 c. extra virgin olive oil
juice of 1 lemon
salt & pepper

For the Radish Cucumber Yogurt
4 red radishes, grated & squeezed dry with a dish towel
1 cucumber, peeled & seeded, grated & squeezed dry with a dish towel
1 clove garlic, minced
1 tbsp. fresh dill, chopped
1 tbsp. fresh oregano, chopped
1/4 c. feta cheese, crumbled fine
1 tsp. cumin
1 c. Greek or unflavored yogurt
salt & white pepper

For the Kofta
1 lb. ground beef
1 lb. ground lamb
1/2 medium yellow onion, minced
1 clove garlic, minced
2 tsp. black pepper
2 tsp. cumin
2 tsp. sumac (for authentic flavor)
1 tsp. fennel seeds
1 tsp. fresh thyme, chopped
1 1/2 tsp. cinnamon
1 tsp. yellow curry powder
1 tsp. crushed red pepper
1 tsp. smoked paprika
1 1/2 tbsp. salt
1/2 c. Moravian Spice Cookies

Kofta

Soy-Sesame Glazed Long Island Duck

Made with Water Chestnut, Scallion, Bok Choy, Spice Cookie Stuffing

For the Stuffing

Sauté the vegetables in a sauté pan over medium high heat. Deglaze with soy and hoisin sauce. Prepare according to stuffing mix directions with chicken broth. Add the Moravian Spice Cookies and sautéed vegetables to the stuffing mix. Bake according to directions.

For the Marinade and Duck

Stir all ingredients in the marinade together and soak the duck in the marinade overnight (at least 24 hours). Remove the duck and place in a large roasting pan. Roast at 400° for 30-35 minutes. Remove duck from the oven, separate legs from carcass, and place legs in a nonstick sauté pan skin side down. Place back in the oven at 350° for 1 1/2 hours, loosely covered with aluminum foil. Once legs are crispy and tender, remove from the oven. While legs finish cooking, cut breasts from the duck and place in a hot sauté pan over medium high heat. Dry sear the breast skin side down for 12-15 minutes. Once the fat has rendered and the skin has crisped, flip over briefly to sear other side and let rest 8 minutes.

For the Plating

Serve some of the sliced breast meat with a portion of the crispy leg. Serve over stuffing with hoisin sauce on the side.

Ingredients

For the Stuffing
1 sm can sliced water chestnuts
5 scallions, sliced thin
1 lrg head bok choy, sliced
1 c. shiitake mushrooms, sliced
2 tbsp. soy sauce
1 tsp. hoisin sauce
1 sm pack stuffing mix
1/2 c. Moravian Spice Cookie
  Crumbles
1 c. chicken broth

For the Marinade
2 c. soy sauce
4 cloves garlic, crushed
1 tbsp. sesame oil
1 c. brown sugar
1/4 c. rice wine vinegar
2 c. water

For the Duck
One 5 - 6 lb. Long Island duck

Soy-Sesame Glazed Duck